LOST COLLECTOR CARS
ALONG THE MOTHER ROAD

ROUTE 66

BARN FIND

ROAD TRIP

TOM COTTER

PHOTOGRAPHY BY
MICHAEL ALAN ROSS

Brimming with creative inspiration, how-to projects, and useful information to enrich your everyday life, Quarto Knows is a favorite destination for those pursuing their interests and passions. Visit our site and dig deeper with our books into your area of interest: Quarto Creates, Quarto Cooks, Quarto Homes, Quarto Lives, Quarto Drives, Quarto Explores, Quarto Gifts, or Quarto Kids.

This edition published in 2019 by Crestline,
an imprint of The Quarto Group
142 West 36th Street, 4th Floor
New York, NY 10018 USA
T (212) 779-4972 **F** (212) 779-6058
www.QuartoKnows.com

First published in 2016 by Motorbooks, an imprint of The Quarto Group, 100 Cummings Center, Suite 265-D, Beverly, MA 01915, USA.

Crestline titles are also available at discount for retail, wholesale, promotional, and bulk purchase. For details, contact the Special Sales Manager by email at specialsales@quarto.com or by mail at The Quarto Group, Attn: Special Sales Manager, 100 Cummings Center Suite 265D, Beverly, MA 01915, USA.

10 9 8 7 6 5 4 3 2 1

ISBN: 978-0-7858-3749-7

Acquiring Editor: Zack Miller
Project Manager: Jordan Wiklund
Art Director: Brad Springer
Cover Designer: Kent Jensen
Layout Designer: Brad Norr
Layout: Rebecca Pagel

On the front cover: The 1949 Ford was heralded as the beginning of Ford's new era after World War II. More than sixty years later, this '49 Ford is waiting for its own new era to begin.
On the endpapers: Vintage Route 66 postcards. *Motorbooks collection*
On the frontis: "On A Hill Far Away Stands An Old Chevrolet" by Dan McCrary (*dmccraryart.com*)

Printed in China

CONTENTS

ACKNOWLEDGMENTS

Many folks made this ambitious book possible.

I always end these acknowledgment pages thanking my wife, Pat, so this time I'm starting with her. Babe, thanks for letting me leave for nearly four weeks while you handled all the household chores. I'm back now, so I'll bring out the garbage and make the bed for a while.

Thank you to everyone who helped us along the way: owners of cars we found, folks who gave us leads on barn-finds, and those who sent us leads on social media. We wouldn't have found as many cars without your help.

Thanks to everyone at Motorbooks/Quarto Publishing—Zack Miller, Nichole Schiele, Jordan Wiklund, and everyone else who in some way touched my book, from editing to design to production, delivering, and warehousing. I can't believe that you keep endorsing these crazy book ideas.

Thanks to new barn-finding partner, Hagerty Insurance, who allowed Claire Walters, Ben Woodworth, and Jordan Lewis to follow us with video cameras for a new YouTube barn-finding series, *Barn Find Hunter*.

Thank you to Ford Motor Company, which gave us a brand new 2016 Explorer for Michael to drive as our support vehicle and luggage hauler. If I needed to buy a new SUV, it would be an Explorer, without a doubt.

And thanks to you readers who believe there is always a worthy car around the next corner. I promise to keep writing these books if you keep buying them!

Happy hunting!

—*Tom*

Two Ford SUVs, seventy-seven years apart!

PHOTOGRAPHER'S NOTES

We've all experienced game-changers. For me, one of those moments was asking Tom Cotter for five minutes of his time. It's been a whirlwind ever since—we've traveled thousands of miles, met hundreds of people, and found thousands of cars. Hell, we've even partied with rock stars!

So when the phone rings and it's Tom Cotter, you never know what could happen next. It could be sharing a new story or the beginning of a new adventure. After completing *Barn Find Road Trip*, the spiritual predecessor to this book, Tom and I started thinking about our next project. One day Tom called and said, "I've got it." When he asked if I'd be interested in doing a sequel on Route 66 from beginning to end, I went all in. As a seven-year-old, I'd traveled Route 66 in the back of a '59 Chevy station wagon and the memories are still etched in my mind.

From playing the license plate game to counting hundreds of box cars with my brothers, and certainly the look on my father's face somewhere in Arizona as he experienced his third flat tire in one day. The Mother Road is a part of me.

The opportunity of discovering Route 66 from beginning to end and to tell the story with my camera was something I couldn't turn down. We pushed every day from dawn 'til dusk and then some. There is no rest for a "Cotter Spotter."

If there's one thing I've learned from doing trips like this, it's that the most rewarding thing is not the "best find," it's the people we meet along the way. We heard stories from perfect strangers that touched us to the core, as if we'd known them for years. Sure, the cars are cool, but without the stories and the faces, they're just another catalyst for a tetanus shot.

I hope you enjoy this book as much as we enjoyed that burger in Sapulpa, Oklahoma, and experiencing dawn at the Cadillac Ranch in Amarillo. I encourage you to go out and embrace this BIG gorgeous country. Bring a camera, make conversation with a stranger, and enjoy the smile of a waitress in the middle of nowhere as she serves you that last piece of blueberry pie à la mode.

There's nothing better than the open road to clear your head. Who knows—it might just be your next game-changer.

—Michael Alan Ross

NAVIGATIONAL NOTES

Sterling Moss and Denis Jenkinson. Tom Cotter and Brian Barr. That's a stretch, but being a good navigator requires having a great driver. Tom has given me that opportunity, first in *Barn Find Road Trip* and now in *Route 66 Barn Find Road Trip*.

Most important is communication. This means being able to translate directional instructions given in grunts, groans, hand signals, waving, nods, and, sometimes, words.

A good map and atlas are essential. Invest in detailed versions. We used *Route 66: The Map Series* by Jim Ross and *EZ66: Route 66 Guide* for Travelers, by Jerry McClanahan. Both are excellent and give pre- and postwar routes.

While technology is a not a necessity, it can enhance the Route 66 experience. As the hobby evolves, it makes sense barn-finders use the best technology available to them to find future stashes of rusty Vipers, WRXs, and Mustang GTs.

We used MyTracks GPS Tracking App. Dropping pins at every location so we had the GPS coordinates made it easy to identify sites and track mileage. Google Earth and Maps let us look beyond the highway when our instincts were low or topography blocked our view. We pinpointed our social media leads and used GPS to find them.

Technology has been with us through every journey we take. After all, Jenks created the first rally route navigation tool from a roll of toilet paper . . . just saying.

—Brian Barr

A few days before leaving for our trip, Michael Alan Ross, our photographer, sent an email half-joking that we should buy a snake-bite kit because we'd be spending time in the desert. I sent an email back saying that we'd only need a snake-bite kit if we discovered a Cobra.

Then I remembered last year when a pit bull clamped his jaws around my knee while I was looking at a Falcon Ranchero in West Virginia. I thought he was going to tear off my kneecap.

"Good idea, Michael," I later wrote. "Yes, let's buy one, just in case." We had been planning the Route 66 Barn Find Road Trip for months. During the spring, my copilot, Brian Barr, and I drove my Cobra from Charlotte, North Carolina, to McPherson, Kansas, for the annual McPherson College advisory board meeting. During that trip, we went out of our way to drive about 50 miles on Route 66.

During that trip, we met a dynamic English couple that had flown from London to Austin, Texas, and picked up their recently purchased 1974 Starsky and Hutch paint scheme Ford Torino. They told us they would be living the American dream by driving Route 66 from Chicago to LA for the next three weeks.

At the end of our Kansas trip, I called my publisher, Zack Miller, and told him I thought Route 66 might be an ideal follow-up to *Barn Find Road Trip*. I felt it would not only be a car-finding book, but also a travel guide for folks who desired to drive the famous route.

As we did before our previous trip, Brian and I visited the Bagel Bin Deli in Huntersville, North Carolina. We ate hearty breakfast bagels and hit the road toward Chicago before 7 a.m. on Friday, October 30, 2015.

We hit the road from Chicago on Sunday, November 1, letting America's Highway be our guide.

As is our tradition, Brian Barr (right rear) and I again began our road trip with a hearty breakfast from Bagel Bin in Huntersville, North Carolina. "Bin Girls" Vanessa Hughesman (bottom left) and sisters Ronetta (lower center) and Tameka Nelson wished us good luck.

INTRODUCTION

Route 66—the Mother Road. One of the most storied roads in the world, Route 66 has been represented for more than fifty years in books, television, music, all dedicated to that famous stretch of pavement.

If that road could talk, what could it tell us? What famous people traveled that road? How many families from the East began new lives on the West Coast by making a pilgrimage on Route 66? And which makes and models of old cars remain on or near Route 66 in the small towns that dot the route, now that various interstate highways have put many of those towns out of business?

Michael Alan Ross and Brian Barr—my friends and cohorts in the book *Barn Find Road Trip*—were game to find out.

My '39 Ford Woody wagon hit the road on November 1 for a trip totaling nearly 6,000 miles. We scheduled fifteen days to drive from Chicago to the Santa Monica Pier, then three days to return back to Chicago along the interstate system.

I am still amazed that one ribbon of road connects the hustle-and-bustle city of Chicago to the vacant deserts of New Mexico. It's an amazing transformation, from chrome-and-glass skyscrapers to sixty-year-old art-deco gas stations and hotels, all leading to the pier in the Pacific beachside town of Santa Monica.

We met amazing people and heard amazing stories along the way. We found an amazing number of cars. Most of them are for sale, some are restorable, and some are drivers as-is. And, alas, some are so rusty or stripped they can only be classified as parts cars or yard art.

Even though I don't need another car, there were a couple that easily could have followed me home. But I'd need to find a new place to live if I dragged home another barn-find . . .

It was an amazing adventure for a couple of old car guys. Sorry, there was not enough room in the Woody for you to come along for the ride, but hopefully this book will feel like you were sitting in the passenger seat.

Buckle up and enjoy the ride—it's a great country!

—*Tom Cotter*

ROUTE 66

ILLINOIS

SUNDAY, NOVEMBER 1, 2015

We had hoped to be on the road early Sunday morning, but it was noon before we actually started heading west. My friend Lou Natenshon and his wife, Abbie, invited the three of us—Michael Alan Ross, our photographer; Brian Barr, my copilot; and me—to stay at their house in the Chicago suburb of Highland Park the night before our departure. We jumped at this offer, not only because it saved us hotel expenses for one night, but also because we would have the opportunity to see Lou's car collection. Lou's garage holds a fantastic selection of cars, which includes everything from a 1934 Ford Indy racer to a V8-60 MGTF vintage racer and a bright yellow Iso Grifo.

· · · · · · · ·

Lou told me there was a cars and coffee event just north of his home in Lake Forest the next morning and suggested we attend before hitting the road. I agreed, thinking we might develop a lead on some old cars we could follow up during our trip. Knowing Chicago occasionally experiences brief, brutal, and severe early winters, we feared snow on this, the first day of November, Day 1 of the Route 66 Barn Find Road Trip. Instead the day dawned as a fabulous, sunny autumn morning.

The Woody had fine company at Lou and Becky Natenshon's house the night before we departed for California. Lou's collection (left to right) includes a Canary Yellow Iso Grifo with a 327, a Jaguar XK120, and a 1963 Porsche 356.

Sunday, November 1 dawned as a spectacular autumn morning—the perfect day to begin a cross-country journey. We headed out of the Natenshons' driveway en route to a cars and coffee event.

ROUTE 66

MILEAGE CHART

ROUTE 66

CHICAGO, ILLINOIS TO

SPRINGFIELD, IL	200	TUCUMCARI, NM	1167
ST. LOUIS, MO	296	NEWKIRK, NM	1199
MULE TRADING POST		SANTA ROSA, NM	1222
ROLLA, MO	401	ALBUQUERQUE, NM	1341
SPRINGFIELD, MO	511	GRANTS, NM	1416
JOPLIN, MO	583	FLAGSTAFF, AZ	1661
TULSA, OK	691	WILLIAMS, AZ	1695
OKLAHOMA CITY, OK	800	SELIGMAN, AZ	1737
CLINTON, OK	885	HACKBERRY, AZ	1787
ELK CITY, OK	910	KINGMAN, AZ	1809
SAYRE, OK	926	OATMAN, AZ	1837
SHAMROCK, TX	961	NEEDLES, CA	1870
MCLEAN, TX	983	BARSTOW, CA	2107
AMARILLO, TX	1056	VICTORVILLE, CA	2157
VEGA, TX	1125	LOS ANGELES, CA	2248
ADRIAN, TX	1139	SANTA MONICA, CA	2278

"GET YOUR KICKS ON ROUTE 66"

Our host for the last evening, Lou Natenshon, enjoying a brisk morning at the FuelFed cars and coffee event. I mean, what man in his right mind would invite three car guys to stay overnight at his house? I know Lou through the small, but active, Cunningham community.

◆ FUELFED ON SUNDAY MORNING ◆

The cars and coffee event was called FuelFed, and the high-end cars in the parking lot reflected the affluence of this community. As opposed to all the late-model Mustangs that populate the monthly Cars and Coffee in the Charlotte, North Carolina, area where I live, FuelFed attracts cars as diverse as Alfa Romeo Giuliettas and even a Zagato-bodied Maserati.

We saw cool cars and actually sniffed out a lead from one of the participants, Sam Danenberger, who drove his Lancia Fulvia. He said his father, Bo, who lived south in Danvers, Illinois, had some interesting foreign cars we might like to see. When we met Bo, we discovered that his son's automotive interests didn't fall far from father's automotive tree.

ROUTE 66

BACK TO THE FUTURE, TWICE

When we drove from Charlotte to Chicago, we had to set our clocks back one hour to adjust for Central Standard Time. Then, because it was Saturday, November 1, it was time to "fall back" an hour. That's two free hours! It made me wonder: if I kept jumping back an hour at a time, could I become thirty years old again?

The folks attending FuelFed gathered around the Woody to ask questions about our trip and to bid us good luck.

The FuelFed gathering attracted an amazing assortment of cars, from hot rods to sports cars to the styling prototype . . .

. . . This amazing 1955 Zagato Maserati Coupe, owned by Joe Hayes, was one of the extraordinary cars that attended FuelFed on Sunday morning.

So with Bo's phone number in hand, we headed south from Lake Forest toward Chicago to officially begin our adventure.

◆ CHICAGO DOGS IN THE WINDY CITY ◆

We actually had two more stops to make before we could hit the road. One was to fill a bottle with Lake Michigan water that we planned to pour into the Pacific Ocean at the conclusion of our trip. We found a beautiful

Pure, one hundred percent authentic Lake Michigan water! I nearly fell in the lake trying to retrieve it. I figured I would ceremoniously pour it into the Pacific Ocean when we reached the Santa Monica Pier in two weeks.

The water was cold, the ladder was rusty, and my grip was failing as I dipped a bottle into Lake Michigan to collect a few ounces of clean and clear Lake Michigan H_2O.

lakefront public park just north of the city bustling with people on this beautiful day. I walked to a dock and located a rusty, rather fragile ladder, and climbed down to fill the bottle. I was nervous—not because of all the people watching, but because I thought I might lose my grip or the ladder would break while I was retrieving the water. But it all worked out and we were soon on our way to stop number two.

If we were going to live the authentic Route 66 experience, we needed to eat local foods along the way to Santa Monica. Starting with one of Chicago's world-famous hot dogs was a necessity.

After retrieving the water but before departing on our journey, we had to sample some of Chicago's finest. Disguised as McDowell's, Wiener Circle is famous for their Chicago dogs.

Brian once lived in Chicago and suggested we eat at a local landmark known as the Wiener Circle. He said that because the day before was Halloween, the famous hot dog stand would still be decorated in its annual "costume" as McDowell's Hot Dogs, a tribute to the Eddie Murphy movie *Coming to America*.

The dogs were good. All three of us ordered them loaded with tomato, relish, onion, pepper, pickle, and mustard. We ate them quickly, and because Route 66 is bumpy, we were reminded of how our lunch tasted even several hours later. "It's all part of the experience," Brian said.

This is what a fully loaded Chicago dog looks like. The nice thing about a hot dog like this is that you can enjoy the taste of it when you eat it and again about an hour later . . .

From the Wiener Circle, we drove to downtown Chicago. Route 66 officially begins across from Grant Park. There, in the middle of one of the most bustling cities in the world, sits a sign near the intersection of Lakeshore Drive and Jackson. "Route 66 Begins Here," it declares. And so shall we.

We parked the Woody next to the sign for a photo op. Had we been driving a generic sedan, we would have been chased away by the building doorman who was stationed nearby. But because we had a seventy-six-year-old wooden automobile and a photographer, with all his professional camera gear, we were allowed to park there that Sunday morning.

Michael took his photos and we were soon off on the Mother Road, the world-renowned famous Route 66. We would spend the next two weeks on and around this famous hunk of asphalt.

◆ ON THE ROAD AGAIN ◆

STARTING MILEAGE: 24,649 MILES

We left the Route 66 sign at 11:49 a.m. on Sunday, November 1, 2015. The Woody's odometer read 24,649 miles. Because it was Sunday, we were not optimistic that we'd actually find old cars within the Chicago city limits. But we'd give it our best shot.

From our experience during last year's road tour, we realized Sundays—especially Sunday mornings—are a tough time to search for old cars.

As we left the Windy City, Route 66 was clearly marked with signs. Some states, we would find, did not honor the great ribbon of asphalt that zigzagged through their state as much as others. Illinois, however, proudly marked the route from its beginning at Grant Park until crossing the McKinley Bridge into St. Louis.

We saw many auto repair shops within the city limits, some with a sampling of old cars sitting on the back of the property. The gates were closed, however, and nobody was around, so we just kept driving.

CAR COUNT 8	FOR SALE
	☐ Yes ★ No ☐ Maybe

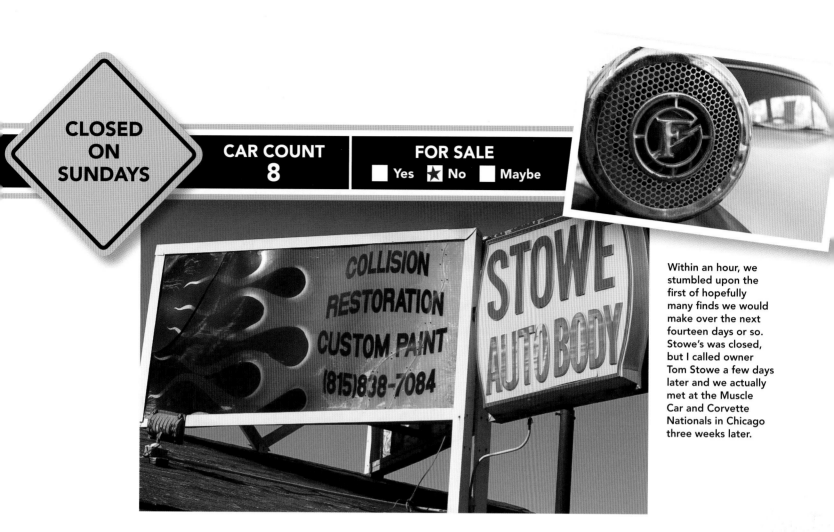

Within an hour, we stumbled upon the first of hopefully many finds we would make over the next fourteen days or so. Stowe's was closed, but I called owner Tom Stowe a few days later and we actually met at the Muscle Car and Corvette Nationals in Chicago three weeks later.

About forty miles into our trip, we came across a shop called Stowe Auto Body, in Lockport, Illinois. Even though the shop was closed and the gates were locked, we could see intriguing metal shapes behind the fence. I called owner Tom Stowe a few days later and he told me about the cars and his business.

"Since 1979, I've been doing frame-off restorations and soda-blasting," Stowe said, whose daily driver is a 1955 Chevy Cameo pickup. "Right now we're restoring a 1928 Hendrickson semitruck for the Hendrickson trucking company."

He explained that the old cars scattered around his property were his own. Some he has owned for as long as forty-five years. And they were not for sale, "although everything can be for sale, I guess," he said.

I asked him about the Bentley sedan that I saw resting on the other side of the fence. "I bought that when my daughter was in eighth grade; now she's forty-four years old," he said. Stowe mentioned that a wrist pin in the engine broke soon after he purchased it, so he just parked it. "One of these days I'll fix it up with a small-block Chevy for my wife," he said.

Since Stowe's is closed on Sundays, all the photos Michael was able to shoot were either over or through the fence. This Bentley has a blown engine, so one day it will probably become a Chevy-powered hot rod for Stowe's wife.

Stowe's personal passion is for early Chevy Apache pickup trucks and Suburbans. In fact, he drives one every day. This is his private collection of future projects and parts trucks.

Former or future hippie van? An employee at Stowe's inherited this VW microbus from his father, who bought it in 1968. With the value of these early split-window buses increasing into the six figures lately, one can only hope that he restores it to its original splendor.

We saw other cars through his closed fence too. We spied a 1957 Chevy convertible. "I bought that one from the brother of the original owner, who was eighty-four," he explained. "I don't know what I'll do with that car yet. I hope to get it into the shop and inspect it over the winter and figure out what I'm going to do."

What about the VW microbus that was sitting next to the door? "That one belongs to a kid who works for me," Stowe said. "His father bought it in 1968. He's thinking about what to do with it."

Stowe also had a number of Chevy Apache and GMC pickups and at least one vintage Suburban behind the fence. Before I said goodbye to him on our phone call, Stowe mentioned that his restoration shop is a favorite pit stop for European travelers. He said that his shop has even been featured in a German book about Route 66. *Interesting*, I thought. Now, he'll be in an American one.

INTERNATIONAL INTRIGUE

CAR COUNT	FOR SALE		
1	★ Yes	No	Maybe

Just a few miles from Stowe's Auto Body, we passed a nice International pickup truck on the side of the road with a "For Sale" sign on it. I don't know much about Internationals, but this truck was extremely nice. It had a 1200-series emblem on it. We opened the hood, revealing a V-8 engine, two-barrel carb, and a four-speed trans. The paint

This International pickup was parked on the side of the road near Stowe's with a "for sale" sign posted on the windshield. With a nice, solid body and paint job, V-8, and four-speed, the truck appears that it could easily become someone's daily driver.

looked like it had been applied fairly recently, and the truck appeared to run as-is.

A few more miles up the road in Gardner, Illinois, I noticed an old pickup truck nesting in a driveway. We made the first of probably hundreds of U-turns during the course of our two-week journey and doubled back to find out about the truck. I met owner Jerry Lankford and his family, who were spending a lazy Sunday afternoon sitting in comfortable chairs in their garage, just waiting for a couple of curious barn-finders to stop by.

UNFINISHED DODGY HOT ROD

CAR COUNT	FOR SALE		
1	☐ Yes	★ No	☐ Maybe

Lankford recently regained ownership of the truck and hopes to install a late-model Dodge drivetrain and to drive it again in the next year.

"It's a 1946 Dodge," he said. "I bought it in 1977 for $275.

It needed brakes and rear fenders. I brought it home, worked on it for two weeks, and had it on the road and drove it for a while. Then my son tried to make a hot rod out of it, and he ruined it. He took out the original drivetrain and put in a 302 Ford engine and a C6 tranny."

Jerry is clearly bitter about what happened to the truck after he sold it to his son. "He never did drive it," he said. "He just let it sit here and go to hell."

When we inspected the truck in the fall of 2015, it had been sitting in Lankford's driveway for about a quarter-century. A few years ago, his son's daily driver broke down, so Jerry worked out a swap that he would trade

A sad Ford-powered Mopar, Jerry Lankford's 1946 Dodge pickup sits forlorn in his driveway in Gardner, Illinois, awaiting attention. Lankford drove the truck for many years before his son attempted to convert it to Ford 302 power. He never finished it, so it sits.

his late-model Ford pickup and get his old Dodge back. "I'm going to start working on it again this winter," he said. "It's a Dodge; I'm going to put a Dodge back in it. I think a 360 engine with fuel injection. Everyone wants me to put a new front-end clip on it, but I'm going to keep it stock. I don't care about how it rides—I want it stock. I still really like the truck."

We bid the Lankfords goodbye and continued our journey west toward Los Angeles.

VINTAGE GAS

In Dwight, Illinois, our Route 66 tour book promised we would be treated to a vintage Texaco gas station. The building is beautifully restored and acts as a mini-museum for Route 66 travelers. On the November Sunday when we visited, the station was closed for the season. But in the summer, the station is open for tourists to visit. I noticed a Model T Ford on display in the service bay.

This was the first of many restored gas stations we would see over the next couple of weeks. Many of these buildings were built in the art-deco style and have been restored as such to keep the memory and spirit of Route 66 alive in small towns that were long ago bypassed by interstate highways. These are fantastic, though the sad truth is that many of the original Route

66 gas stations have been closed for years and are collapsing along sections of the Mother Road, ignored by tourists and historians alike.

As we were driving toward our Bloomington hotel near the end of our first day on the road, we passed another station, this one under the Standard Oil banner. It made for a beautiful evening photo session.

This restored Texaco station-turned-tourist attraction in Dwight, Illinois, was the first of many such stations we would see in small towns all along the Route 66 highway during our second barn-find road trip.

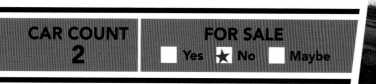

HIPPIE BUS BARN

CAR COUNT	FOR SALE
2	☐ Yes ★ No ☐ Maybe

Passing through Dwight, Illinois, Brian and I noticed a vintage VW microbus partially hidden in a garage with two guys drinking beer next to it. We met the VW's owner, Bob Castillo, and his friend and fellow car guy Steve Anderson. They both work for the nearby Exxon oil refinery, and both were on a fourteen-days-on, one-day-off work shift.

"We're refitting the refinery with new equipment and for maintenance," Anderson said. "Once the fitting is completed, we'll go back to our four ten-hour days, with Fridays, Saturdays, and Sundays off." Then the two car enthusiasts can get back to their projects, which have been on hold.

Bob Castillo, whose home we were visiting, is a longtime VW enthusiast. "I've had this bus for about ten years," Castillo said. "I drove it to work a couple of times. Once after work, a guy I worked with and I stopped and got a six-pack of beer. We figured that if the cops chased us, it

Castillo looks too tough to be into Volkswagens, but they are his automotive passion. The bus will be used for overnight sleeping accommodations when he goes fishing.

As we whizzed around a curve at 40 miles per hour, this scene caught our attention at the end of a 100-foot driveway. It's a VW van that Bob Castillo has owned and fiddled with for the past ten years.

would be like that slow O. J. Simpson Ford Bronco chase scene because this VW doesn't go very fast."

He said that he's working on it to use when he goes fishing. "If it starts getting late, I can just stay that night in the van," he said. Castillo said he has begun doing some bodywork on the Volkswagen. The floors are solid, but both quarter panels needed some work. "It's not for sale," he added.

Castillo guided us to a barn on the rear of his property to show us another of his VW projects. As we entered the barn, I noticed it was a Beetle he was converting into a Baja Bug. A Baja Bug is a Beetle with the front and rear body sections shaved off for more efficient off-roading.

I have a warm place in my heart for Baja Bugs; in 1972, I built a homemade version when I was a senior in high school out of my father's 1959 Beetle that he purchased new. The only thing was, I couldn't afford the fiberglass kit to properly finish off the front and rear ends, so I faked it the best I could by shaping the metal with a jigsaw and installing Model A Ford headlights.

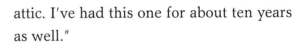

Castillo told me his VW was a 1966. "I have a Type 4 VW engine that I will put in it," he said. "I also have all the Baja Bug fiberglass pieces in the attic. I've had this one for about ten years as well."

Castillo also owns this '66 VW Beetle, which he is slowly turning into a Baja Bug. He recently restored and sold a 1974 Super Beetle, which he hopes will allow him to now spend time on his other projects.

We even learned we have a common connection—barn-finding! "I like to stop and look at old cars when I'm driving down the road too," he said, "but whenever I do that, my wife asks me, 'You're not thinking about buying another one, are you?'"

The sun was dipping low on the horizon as we finished talking with Castillo about his VWs. Steve Anderson, however, asked if we'd like to come over to his house, just a mile or two away, to see his cars.

A FEVER FOR FORDS

CAR COUNT	FOR SALE
4	Yes No ★ Maybe

Above: Anderson is building his '65 Ford Econoline pickup as an old-school drag-type truck. Out goes the six-cylinder, in goes the 302 cubic-inch engine and big wheels to become a Ford version of a Little Red Wagon.

Left: Anderson poses next to the only car he would consider selling—an engineless 1970 Ford Torino that he would let go for $1,500.

"I just live near the old women's prison," Anderson told us. I don't know anything about old women's prisons; is that where elderly female criminals live? But I said I'd love to see his cars.

We followed Anderson's Honda a few miles when we passed what must have been the prison, which appeared to have been shuttered a long time ago. The land was heavily treed over and had not been landscaped for many years. It was obviously out of business. Many industrial-type buildings were at the huge facility, but the building in front—probably the administration building—was a gorgeous piece of architecture. The building was probably one hundred years old and had a friendly, almost whimsical look about it, which I thought was odd when you consider the nature of the building itself, and what may have transpired behind those walls.

Another mile up the road and we found ourselves in Anderson's driveway. It was obvious that he was not into VWs like his friend. He was a Ford man, and we could see several on his property. The car we approached first was an old Falcon Ranchero sitting in his carport. "It's a 1964," he said.

Anderson says this solid 1969 Ford Torino is his winter project. The 351 Windsor will receive a mild hop-up, but otherwise, the car will simply be a nice, nearly fifty-year-old driver.

I noticed the California plates. "Is this an original California car?" I asked.

"Yes, but unfortunately it's not rust-free," he said. "The guy who owned it left the windows down and the floors rusted out. I got it from a guy in Chicago who told me he acquired the Falcon when it broke down in front of his jobsite. The guy who owned it said he could have the Falcon for free if he just gave him a ride to a hotel."

The car has no engine or transmission, but Anderson has plans for that. "I'm going to drop in a Ford big-block," he said. "I have a 460-cubic-inch bored out to 512. It's covered up in the garage. I think I'll put a C6 transmission behind it."

Anderson's plans are to build the car into a gasser-type dragster with a straight-front axle. "It'll have leaf-spring suspension in the front and rear, with skinny wheels up front and fat ones in the back," he said. "When this Ranchero is done, it will scare women and children."

But before he can start scaring people, he had another vehicle to complete. "I'll jump on the Ranchero as soon as my Econoline pickup truck is finished."

On the way to see the Econoline, we walked past a 1969 Torino GT. "That one has a 351 Windsor two-barrel with a C4 automatic in it," Anderson said. "This one was running and driving until a couple of years ago when the plastic timing gear jumped. It's a work in progress. I have a four-barrel intake and headers for it. It will be a winter project."

After the Torino, we walked toward the garage attached to Anderson's house, where his Econoline project lived. "I've only had this one for about three months," he said. "It's a 1965. I'm going to put in a 302 and an automatic so I can drive it anytime I want."

He had already installed old-school Crager S/S rims on it. He hopes to have it resemble a Little Red Wagon–type of dragster when it is completed. "The V-8 fits right in," he said. "I just hope it stays between the lines,

because I hear these steer pretty badly." Strangely enough, Anderson plans to keep drum brakes in the front, but will install disc brakes on an 8-inch Ford rear axle. The pickup, which he got near Bloomington, Illinois, seemed to have a pretty solid body.

As we walked around the rear of the property, Anderson said that this next car might be for sale. "I don't have plans for it," he said. "We found this one in the corn crib of a barn about three miles north of here." It was a dark green 1970 Ford Torino GT.

"We had it running within a half-hour, but mice had been in it, so my buddy pulled it all apart, then lost interest, so I bought it," he added. The Torino's body was in poor shape and it didn't have a drivetrain. "I'd let it go for fifteen hundred dollars just the way it is," he said.

Brian mentioned that the car eerily resembled a dark green 1970 Torino we found on our previous trip and documented in the book *Barn Find Road Trip*. He was right—except that car had a 429 engine and a four-speed transmission.

Here's the car that Steve Anderson hopes will make women and children cry. This 1964 Ford Falcon Ranchero is destined for a straight front axle and big-block power as he transforms it into a street gasser.

◆ GOODNIGHT, DAY ONE ◆

We said goodnight to Anderson, but because the sun was going down and the evening light was becoming "magic," as Michael likes to say, we stayed around the back of his property until the sun was completely set.

Our first day on the Route 66 trail had been ideal. We had feared cold weather or even snow when we had planned this trip. Instead, the sky had been clear, the sun was shining, and the temperatures were around 70 degrees. Not what I expected in the Chicago area in November. Also, we had found a number of interesting cars for a Sunday, which is often rare.

We ended our first day in Bloomington, Illinois, where the famous Bloomington Gold

Michael said to go stand by the car, so I did. He says there is about thirty minutes of "magic light" at sunset each evening, so before we left Steve Anderson's house, he shot a bunch of images.

Award had been conceived for the very best vintage Corvettes. We didn't find any 'Vettes, but we had the rest of Route 66 to scour. Michael, Brian, and I were bushed. We checked into a Hampton Inn and searched for a brewpub to celebrate our first day's successes. No doubt tomorrow would be even better.

◆ DAY TWO, ILLINOIS ◆

Somebody had to be the hard ass early on Monday, November 2, so as usual, it was me. Weeks before our trip began, I opened my *2008 Edition Master Road Atlas* and looked at the eight states we'd be passing through to come up with a reasonable travel timetable. Looking at the sections of the country we would be passing through, I decided that we needed to pass from Texas into Oklahoma on Day 7. That would give us one week to get to the Santa Monica Pier outside of LA to stick to our schedule of fourteen days, give or take a detour or two (or three, or four . . .).

To stay on track, we needed to make Illinois a two-day state. Ending Day 1 in Bloomington held us right on target to end Day 2 in St. Louis, Missouri.

At the Chicago FuelFed breakfast we attended on Sunday morning, we got a lead about a man named Bo Danenberger who lived in the little town of Danvers, Illinois. Bo's son, Sam, told us that his father had a unique collection of vintage foreign cars in the carriage house where he lived. We made arrangements the evening before to visit Bo first thing the next morning. We had an early breakfast and headed back north from Bloomington to Danvers, backtracking a little.

A LITTLE PIECE OF FRANCE IN ILLINOIS

CAR COUNT	FOR SALE		
7	☐ Yes	★ No	☐ Maybe

We arrived in front of Danenberger's building, and if I didn't know I was in the middle of Illinois farming country, I would have thought I was in a quaint little French village. The building is a marvelous old piece of masonry built in 1905. The word "Livery" is

painted on the main beam over the front carriage doors, and the front patio was dotted with many colorful potted plants and wildflowers that made the scene resemble a French marketplace. It was a beautiful and appropriate setting to visit an eclectic foreign car collection.

"I went to England many times in the seventies and I always like the mews, the alleys, and the stables," Danenberger said. "So when I was looking for a place to work on my cars about forty years ago, my realtor showed me this place. You don't create this kind of mess overnight, boys," he laughed. "This wasn't staged for your arrival this morning!"

Danenberger grew up in the Bloomington and Normal, Illinois, area. His friends all drove Fords and Chevys in high school, but he was into imports—specifically MGs.

As I walked around his garage, I was amazed at all the little trinkets and treasures Danenberger had hanging on the walls and on shelves. This could truly have been a repair shop in Europe during the 1960s.

Is this France or Illinois? We drove up to this wonderful brick building, knowing that a garage with this much character just had to have wonder vehicles inside.

Bo Danenberger met us at the front of his amazing building in the Illinois countryside. Starting in his teen years, while all his friends were into Fords and Chevys, Danenberger was more interested in foreign cars.

Danenberger showed us his newest acquisition, this wonderful 1959 Lancia Appia, which he found in Indianapolis three years ago. He said he is fascinated by the Lancia's design and beautifully constructed mechanical bits.

Above: Certainly the only Citroën for miles around, this low-mileage DS19 was a "pub-find" in nearby Bloomington. Buying this car fulfilled the desire to own one since the fifties.

Below: His favorite car to listen to and his least favorite to drive! This 1956 Morgan Plus 4 was raced earlier in its life, but now has a more restful life in Danenberger's livery stable.

Above: Coincidentally, Danenberger purchased this spare Appia engine on Craigslist just before buying the car. The narrow V-4 engine has a single cylinder head, surely out-of-the-box thinking for the day.

Below: Wait, there's another Citroën in the garage, this one a big-block DS21. Danenberger doesn't overrestore and pamper these cars, but drives them like they were meant to be driven.

He showed us one of his more recent acquisitions, a 1959 Lancia Appia sedan, which he found about three years ago in Indianapolis. "The owner died thirty-five years ago, and it had sat in the garage ever since," he said. "Mechanically, it was toast. The brakes were frozen, the engine was stuck, it had a whole bunch of problems, but that's my thing."

He said that since new paint and upholstery are expensive, he decided to leave those items alone and just concentrate on the Lancia's mechanicals. "It was on Craigslist," he said. "Oddly enough I have another V-4 Appia

Not a car you see every day, or even every five years! This Renault Dalphine is a tidy and reliable car as long as you don't consider taking it on a cross-country drive! Cute as a button, though.

It's the small details that are easy to overlook in Danenberger's shop—the wonderful hand tools in wooden cabinets and parts and pieces on the shelves—that speak to forty years of constant use.

engine in the back of the shop that I bought off New York Craigslist just two weeks before buying this car. I bought the engine just because it is such a beautiful piece of equipment. The Lancia machine work and design is so wonderful for just being pieces of equipment."

"I only had to rebuild the head on this Lancia," he continued. "I kept soaking and soaking the block, and one day the stuck pistons started to move."

Sitting in the garage near the Lancia were two cars hardly ever seen in America: Citroëns, a 1965 and a 1966. Danenberger said he was a bit of a Citroën nut. "I've wanted one of these since the fifties," he said. "I had a Traction Avant, but I always wanted a D. Once I was coming home from work and this DS19 was sitting behind a tavern in Bloomington. It had only twenty-four thousand miles on the odometer, so I bought it."

Danenberger told me how to identify a DS19 from a DS21. "If it's got quad headlights, it's a two-liter or larger, making it a DS21," he said. "The single-headlight cars have engines smaller than two liters, making those DS19s." One of the more enjoyable aspects of barn-finding is that I learn something new every day.

The car that started the obsession for Danenberger, the MGTD. He's owned this 1953 for nearly a half century, even though he notes that he is not an MG guy, but a car guy.

In the middle of the garage was a yellow 1956 Morgan Plus 4 with a Triumph TR3 motor. "I've had it twelve or fifteen years," Danenberger said. "I bought it from a friend. It was a racer earlier in its life. It's a bad car to drive. There is no room to steer and I have to wear smaller shoes just to work the pedals. I love it because of the car's great sound. It's fast and hairy, but I'd rather drive anything else I have than this car."

Before inspecting the rest of his building, Danenberger drew our attention to a small car in the corner—a Renault Dauphine. "These were much maligned cars when they were new because they were French and they were cheap," he said of the water-cooled 750cc car that was designed to steal sales from the VW Beetle. "They were basically junk. But this 1960 has become quite a nice little car. It belonged to a local school teacher. You can see the driver's door has quite a bong in it. Someone hit her in a shopping center parking lot and she parked the car in the garage and never drove it again. It's a piddler; I can go out into the country for a short drive, but I just can't drive it everywhere."

Danenberger told us his theory of auto repair on the road. "I don't do it," he said. "I once bought a Peerless in England in the mid-1970s, had it shipped to Baltimore, and decided to drive it back here to Danvers. I made it, but if I didn't, I would have just called a rollback. I didn't take a single tool. I've learned you don't tinker with a car out on the road. You can't be a hero." (I respectfully disagree—the field repairs we made on the Woody during the first Barn Find Road Trip allowed us to complete the trip in our two-week time frame and deliver the manuscript to the publisher on time!)

"One day, my son Sam called and said that his Lancia had died," Danenberger added. "'Dad, it died, it died.' I said, 'What's the issue?'"

"'I went over some railroad tracks and it just died.'"

"I recommended that he check the coil wire and the plug wires. Then I asked, 'Is there a coffee shop nearby? Yes? Then go get a cup of coffee and it will start when you are done.' I can't explain it, but it's a true story. It's like a fart in the wind—it started right up!"

The only car we hadn't discussed was his MGTD, which had been part of his life for a long time. "It's a 1953," he said. "I've had it since 1959. It was my only car for years, winter and summer. I have pictures of it on rallies with snow and ice all over it."

Danenberger has owned a number of MGs: an MGA, a Magnette, and an Arnolt MG, but he's quick to point out, "I'm not necessarily an MG guy. I'm a Lancia guy, a Ferrari guy, a Jaguar guy . . . I'm just a car guy mostly interested in import stuff."

It was wonderful to meet Bo Danenberger. He is retired from the nursery and garden center business, which explained the beautiful florals in front of his building. His office is on the ground level and it contains as much automotive memorabilia as the adjacent garage. He keeps his home on the second floor, just above his unique collection.

Almost too accurate to be true, this hand-laid fiberglass body was fabricated by Danenberger's friend in the 1950s without the benefit of a mold. Danenberger hopes to display the car at upcoming Road America vintage races, where it once lapped in anger.

He doesn't like to sell his cars, but he has on occasion. For instance, he sold his Peerless not too long ago. "If someone needs to have something, they can, but I'm certainly not in this for the money," he said.

When he mentioned that he had a race car upstairs—in the kitchen of his second apartment!—we told him we had to see it. On the way upstairs, we discussed a photo he had of a Cunningham racing at Road America at Elkhart Lake, Wisconsin, in 1955.

The crème-de-la-crème of the Danenberger collection was what awaited us upstairs, this small-scale Jaguar D-type-appearing, Crosley-powered H-Modified race car that was like a piece of jewelry.

It's hard to miss the big hot dog man when driving into the town of Atlanta, Illinois. It's one of the first towns since leaving Chicago to truly embrace the Route 66 heritage, with a museum, a restaurant, and other businesses that cater to tourists.

"I met Briggs," he said. "I just walked up to him in the paddock at Road America and introduced myself. He was just that kind of guy. Then, when Briggs moved his entire car collection from the northeast to the Costa Mesa museum in the 1960s, his crew chief Alfred Momo and two transporters came hauling his collection right through the little town of Normal, where I lived. There were two open transporters being fueled downtown with Bugattis and the rest of his collection right out there in the open."

Danenberger's race car had belonged to a friend of his, Bruce Thompson, who built and raced the car in H-Modified class at tracks like Road America.

When we reached the top of the stairs, there on the floor was an honest-to-God race car that was a perfectly proportioned 7/8-scale Jaguar D-Type. It was an absolutely beautiful piece of work.

"How my friend Bruce sourced a gated five-speed gearbox in Bloomington in the 1950s, I'll never know," he said. "It's from a Lancia Appia, like the one I have downstairs. This car was raced from roughly 1956 until about 1965. The body is made of fiberglass. I have no idea how Bruce was able to make it so exact without a mold. It was all laid up by hand."

To me, the Crosley-powered racer's chassis resembled a miniature Birdcage Maserati, and made of tiny brazed steel tubes. It was called the TXP, for Thompson X-Perimental. Brian and I salivated over the car as Michael clicked photos of the body and chassis.

"I'm getting ready to bring it to Elkhart Lake for a static display during the vintage racing weekend," Danenberger said. "The plan is to clean it thoroughly because it's been here for thirty-five, maybe forty years. We'll bring it downstairs on the elevator over there."

It had been an amazing couple of hours at Bo Danenberger's. I never would have believed such a collection existed in the middle of farm country. Before leaving, I asked him if he had a favorite car in his collection. He thought for a moment before responding.

"You know, I can't say," he said. "Do I like my son Adam more than I like my son Sam?"

We met Scotsman Peter Friel in Atlanta. The avid cyclist quit his job as a photographer to pedal Route 66. He hoped to make the 2,500-mile journey in about forty days. He either camped out or was the guest of kind people along the route.

◆ WESTWARD HO! ◆

Driving on Route 66 beyond Bloomington, we came across an intriguing little town named Atlanta. Brian read in his travel guide that it was a town worth visiting because there was a Route 66 museum and a few interesting artifacts.

As soon as we parked along Main Street, we met a gentleman on a bicycle who told us his story. He told us his name was Peter Friel, and he lived in Glasgow, Scotland. Friel was pedaling his bicycle from Chicago to LA on Route 66! It was the same route we were traveling, except our trip was scheduled for just two weeks. He planned on pedaling for over a month! Friel, who actually started pedaling in Ottawa, Canada, hoped to ride 80 to 90 miles a day.

He was so intriguing that we offered to buy him lunch in the Palms Grill Café, which was literally the only place to eat in town. "You start hearing about Route 66 in Europe as a kid," Friel told us. "I think Route 66 is more famous in Europe than it is here in the States. I do a lot of riding, so I figured, why not? I quit my job as a photographer to pedal Route 66."

The Palms Grille Café, which originally opened in 1934, before Route 66 and was a household name among motorheads, was an ideal place to eat. Not only was it the only restaurant around, but the food itself was terrific. Our server, Tanya McCarter, told us the original Palms burned down in the 1960s and stayed closed for forty years until the family of the original owner decided to restore it. An original

Our server at the historic Palms Grille in Atlanta, Tanya McCarter. The original Palms burned and sat abandoned for decades before the owner decided to restore the building.

1934 menu was on display that offered "Choice of three meats, two veggies and a drink" for forty-five cents. We paid a bit more than that in 2015, but got a terrific meal in exchange.

I promise you that their cheeseburgers are terrific, crafted from hand-made patties, and their homemade pie—especially the blackberry—would be worth a detour to sample.

Michael and I tried to convince Brian, a bachelor, to consider taking his suitcase out of the Woody and just moving into Atlanta, Illinois, and perhaps settle down with a nice girl like Tanya. But Brian said he was a team player and that he couldn't abandon us on only the second day of our Route 66 tour.

What a guy. What a pie!

SUICIDE DOOR PLYMOUTH	CAR COUNT 1	FOR SALE ☐ Yes ★ No ☐ Maybe

A man named Bill Thomas heard us talk about Route 66 and walked over to our table. I don't know if Thomas is the mayor of Atlanta, but if not, he certainly should be. He and his wife moved there many years ago because they liked the look of the clock tower in the middle of town. He is a retired educator and now runs a few entrepreneurial endeavors in addition to being the chairman of the Route 66 National Steering Committee.

Proud Atlanta business owner and Route 66 spokesman Bill Thomas with his suicide-door Plymouth. Thomas is spearheading an effort for all eight Route 66 states to embrace the historical significance of the once-famous road.

After our meal, Thomas led us outside and showed us his baby, a black 1940 Plymouth Deluxe four-door sedan that he drives daily and parks on Atlanta's main drag, just below his office window. "One day, about twenty-five years ago, I was sitting in my office and it drove up and parked outside," he said. "What sold me on it was the suicide doors. I've always wanted a car with suicide doors. It had a 'For Sale' sign on the window, so I walked outside and bought it."

Over the years, Thomas has had the car repainted and even had the original engine rebuilt by a restorer in Indianapolis. "Now I sit up in my office over there and watch tourists take pictures of it every day," Thomas said. "In our little town of Atlanta, we're trying to re-create an experience for people. And what better way than to have this parked out in the street to help take them back in time?"

Atlanta, Illinois, is a cool town, so after lunch we drove around it for a while before continuing our trek south and west. A mechanic at the local repair shop told us there were a few old cars in peoples' yards just outside of town.

ROUTE 66 NATIONAL STEERING COMMITTEE

"Each international tourist who comes to the US, they don't think of Route 66 as eight separate states—they think of it all as one thing," said Bill Thomas, chairman of the Route 66 National Steering Committee. "So we are creating a new umbrella organization to pull it all together. This is an effort that is long overdue. It's a struggle to bring all the states that Route 66 passes through to coordinate their efforts. Every state has its own Route 66 association, but they don't always work well together."

Thomas said that one of the first initiatives his organization hopes to accomplish is to issue to the US Congress a bill that designates Route 66 as a Historic Trail, and to tie it all together under common signage and federal protection. For updates on the progress of the Route 66 Steering Committee, go to https://sites.google.com/site/66roadahead, or contact Bill Thomas, the Committee Chair, directly at rt66theroadahead@gmail.com

Nobody was home at Ed Craig's house outside of Atlanta, but we stopped to take photos of the cars anyway. Several days later we spoke to Craig on the phone. He said his best cars were in the garages.

Two Comets, a 1963 and a '64, that Craig picked up cheap for small parts to use on his other projects. He'll sell them for $400 each. Sounds like a no-brainer.

A mile or two from town, we noticed a nice farmhouse with a few old cars parked outside—a 1964 Ford Galaxie and two Mercury Comets. We parked the Woody and the Explorer and I knocked on the door. Nobody was home. So we walked back to look at the cars. Before we drove off, I left a note inside the screen door. A few days later, I got a call from Ed Craig, who was calling from his winter home in Florida. He had just left his Atlanta, Illinois, home a couple of days before our arrival. His brother, who lives nearby, discovered the note when he checked on Ed's house the next day.

I asked Craig about the Galaxie and the Comets we saw behind his barn. "I thought you were calling about my nice cars," he said.

I told him I didn't know he had nice cars. I only knew about the cars that were outside.

"I buy old Comets and Falcons when I can, because it's hard to find those parts," he said. "It's also hard to find bumpers for 1963 and 1964 full-size Fords, so when I find a reasonably priced car with good bumpers, I buy it. I bought that '64 from a neighbor who lives about one mile up the road. It has a 289 and a good transmission."

Craig said he would sell the Comets, a 1963 and a '64 (both original), for $400 each. He said he has the titles, but the mice have gotten in and ruined the interiors.

Craig told me that inside the garages he has a very nice 1965 Chevy Impala SS and a two-owner 1950 Ford Tudor. "I bought the Ford from an old woman," he said. "It's black and has an original interior, but I nosed and decked it and installed fourteen-inch wheels."

The seventy-six-year-old retired mailman also farms his 160-acre spread, collects pedal cars and pedal tractors, and even has a 1950 pedal Kidillac. "I also have two complete sets of Illinois license plates from 1912 to 1995," he said. "They are all original, not restored."

GOVERNMENT-CERTIFIED MOTORHOMES

CAR COUNT	FOR SALE
25	★ Yes ☐ No ☐ Maybe

We spotted an unusual sight just a hundred feet or so off Route 66—a field full of vintage motorhomes. We had to find out why they were there.

As we pulled up, a gentleman named Chris Hoagland walked out of his office to greet us. Hoagland told us why he had so many of these intriguing coaches. "These were built by FMC, a government contractor that built vehicles for the US Army," he said. "These were made in Santa Clara, California."

Hoagland explained that when the Vietnam War ended, FMC had huge manufacturing capabilities and skilled craftsmen that the US government wanted to keep in place. So the company was "put" into the business of motor coach manufacturing. In the 1970s, FMC utilized

Chris Hoagland and his father began repairing and selling the unusual coaches decades ago. With about one thousand built, Hoagland's business has pretty much dried up in recent years.

These rigs certainly had a presence! Powered by big-block Chryslers and suspended with the underpinnings of an armored personnel carrier, these motorhomes were the class of the field in the 1970s.

Certainly the most unusual and largest barn-finds we'd come across on this trip. We had to stop and check out this field of FMC motorhomes. The story of these government-funded coaches is probably worthy of a book by itself.

the suspension from its APC113 armored personnel carrier and designed a luxury coach around it. FMC motor coaches were only manufactured for four years, 1973 to 1976. Only 1,050 were built.

"My dad, who passed away in 2008, bought an FMC motor coach new," he said. "When he ruined a front spindle, FMC was out of the motorhome business. So Dad had to have a new one made."

Seeing a business opportunity, Chris's dad started a business to repair and refurbish FMC coaches in the mid-1980s. Hoagland told us that high-end motorhomes in the 1970s sold in the high $30,000 range, but FMCs sold in the high $50,000 range. "Even at that price, someone told my dad that FMC had a hundred thousand dollars invested in each motorhome, that each unit was subsidized by the US taxpayer so that the price could be more competitive."

Each FMC motorhome had a rear-mounted 440 Chrysler industrial engine installed as well as four-wheel independent suspension and a fiberglass body.

The FMC's claim to fame was that Charles Kuralt drove one in his *On the Road* television series. Kuralt's retired FMC now sits in the Henry Ford Museum in Dearborn, Michigan.

"We had a big shop in Lincoln, and when Dad got sick in 2001, I had to take over," Hoagland said. "Our average customer drove fifteen hundred miles one way just to get their vehicle serviced. I made plenty of money in those early days, but I couldn't make enough to support that huge shop and two acres. So we moved the operation down here in Broadwell."

Eventually, the FMC business evaporated. These days, Hoagland will still work on someone's FMC coach or sell them a part, but his income comes primarily from the vehicle repair contract he has with FedEx Ground trucks. "I've got a wife and kids, and there just wasn't enough FMC business to provide me with an income," he said.

He has about twenty-five coaches on his property now, but at one time he said he had twice that many parked here. Most of these coaches were dropped were off at his shop many years ago with the intention of Hoagland selling it on consignment for the owner. But as the vehicles got older and less desirable, they just sat and took root. "These days the FMC repair business is what I call my 'hobby business,'" he said.

Hoagland said that because the vehicles are predominantly fiberglass and aluminum, and the fact that scrap metal values have dropped, the vehicles have no real value. Not all FMCs became motor coaches, though. Hoagland said that 138 were pressed into shuttle duty, sold to companies such as Hertz for use at airports. Some of those are still in use today.

CAR COUNT 4	FOR SALE ☐ Yes ☐ No ★ Maybe

MANTIQUES: ONE WORD SAYS IT ALL

Literally across Route 66 from Chris Hoagland's FMC motor coach graveyard was a sign that said *Mantiques* with an arrow pointing down a road. I knew exactly what the word meant: cool old stuff for guys, so I had to find out more. Unfortunately, nobody was home, but I looked around and peeked in windows the best I could. There was a 1953 Chevy Bel Air and a 1950 Chevy rat rod pickup parked in the yard. I thought there might be cool stuff inside the building, but it was locked. So I left a note on the

Mantiques headquarters! Across the street from Hoagland's FMC graveyard was Ed Deilkes's Mantiques, a unique gift shop that is sure to satisfy the hard-to-please car-guy on your gift list.

door to please call me when possible. A few days later, I received a call from owner Ed Deilkes from Broadwell, Illinois.

"I get home from the bottling plant at 10:30 a.m. and my wife doesn't get home until 6:30 p.m., so I go into the garage and mess around," he said.

He told me about his cars: "The '53 Chevy sedan was a barn-find. A woman owned it, so it's in pretty good shape. It still has the original six-cylinder and three-speed transmission. I'm restoring it little by little. I'm going to install a twin-carb manifold and a split Fenton exhaust. The '50 Chevy pickup has a 350 and a turbo transmission. It has a '77 Buick subframe with full suspension travel, but it's real low."

Besides the cars, Deilkes buys, sells, trades, and collects vintage oil and gas signs. He calls it Man-Junk. "I also make furniture out of old car parts that we sell at flea markets," he said. "Like a lamp with an aluminum cylinder head base and a hubcap for a lampshade."

Besides fabricating cool car-themed gifts, Deilkes has a couple of neat old cars himself, including this slammed 1950 Chevy pickup, which has a complete late-model GM drivetrain and suspension.

Deilkes is also working on this ex-little-old-lady 1953 Chevy, which is destined for dual carbs and a split manifold.

DON'T GO THERE

CAR COUNT	FOR SALE	SCREW HIM—
191	★ Yes ■ No ■ Maybe	**BAD ATTITUDE!**

We passed a business along the interstate with many, many cars, mostly from the mid-sixties and early-seventies era of muscle cars. Nobody was around, so I called the proprietor on the phone. The man said everything was for sale, but he was not interested in talking about the cars, being in our book, or having photographs published.

Unfortunately, I am not at liberty to give you the name or address of this guy's business.

CABOVER KINGDOM

CAR COUNT	FOR SALE
2	Yes ★ No Maybe

Cabover buddies Caldwell (left) and Haywood. By being nicely persistent to an elderly collector, they were able to acquire a couple of trucks that are seldom seen these days.

Driving along Route 66, we saw a couple of rusty old pickup trucks on display at a storage facility in Williamsville, Illinois. We pulled over to take a look, but nobody was on site. Just as we were leaving, a man and a young girl drove up in a BMW 325 convertible. His name was Jason Haywood and he just wanted to look at the Woody for a moment.

"I like your car," he said. He told us he had just picked up his daughter from school. He also said he had just purchased a 1939 Chevy Cabover truck. Now *that* got our attention—since many old trucks were often driven hard and put away wet, few exist today. He told us his truck was apart, but perhaps we would like to see his friend Jack Caldwell. Caldwell owned a similar truck, a 1953 Cabover. We followed his BMW to a storage complex. Caldwell opened the door, revealing the truck inside.

Those early Chevy Cabover trucks (and also the Fords and Dodges) have such presence. They have terrific art-deco influence in their design with many intriguing compound curves. No wonder hot rodders are so enthusiastic about them today.

"About four years ago, we were at an auction and there was an old Marathon fuel tank," Caldwell said. "I bought it for a hundred and fifty dollars and put it out here in front of my shop. Well, this eighty-two-year-old guy comes by and says he's interested in buying it, so I sold it to him, but I had to deliver it to his house. We delivered it up to the town of Goodfield and he opens his barn and we find this truck and Jason's '39."

Caldwell said there were other trucks and cars, wooden bicycles, all sorts of interesting items. He couldn't get the image of those trucks out of his mind. "Then two years ago, I called the man and asked if he still had the trucks, and of course he did," Caldwell said. "This year, I couldn't stand it any longer, so I went back to his house and bought them."

Caldwell said the body and floors of his truck are amazingly solid. The 1953 Chevy has a four-speed gearbox with a two-speed axle. "First gear is such a granny gear that I don't know how you could get from first to second without the truck coming to a complete stop," he said. "The old guy had a pile of parts that came with the truck, so we're just going through those pieces now. We just got the truck three months ago. I would really love to find a small pickup box to put on the back."

Jason Haywood's 1939 Chevy Cabover came from the same gentleman. He plans to keep the exterior original but install a late-modern Cummings diesel.

The unusual discovery of two Cabovers was the perfect way to end the second day of our adventure. We were not quite out of Illinois so we

Jason Haywood introduced us to his friend Jack Caldwell, who owns this killer 1953 Chevy Cabover. The recently purchased truck is being cleaned up and one day will have some type of commercial body installed.

thought we'd stay near the state line that night, putting us within spitting distance of the Mississippi River, and St. Louis, Missouri, the next morning.

"Boys, it's almost beer-thirty," I said.

But then we saw the sign.

COUNTRY CLASSIC CARS— A COLLECTION FOR A COLLECTOR

CAR COUNT 640	FOR SALE ★ Yes ☐ No ☐ Maybe

We had received a few tips from people along the route saying we needed to stop at Country Classic Cars along the interstate. With the sun already set, we passed a field of old cars and a sign saying they had 640 cars in stock!

We exited the interstate, but as we drove to the front gate, the staff was getting ready to lock up for the evening. So we decided to get a hotel in nearby Litchfield and come back first thing in the morning to visit Country Classic Cars. This would prevent us from reaching St. Louis that evening, but for 640 cars, it was worth the delay.

◆ DAY THREE: ILLINOIS ◆

Country Classic Cars sits along I-55 on 13 acres in Staunton, Illinois, just north of the Missouri state line. If you are an old car guy, you shouldn't miss it. As you pass by on the interstate, you'll see dozens of old cars. But that's just the tip of the iceberg.

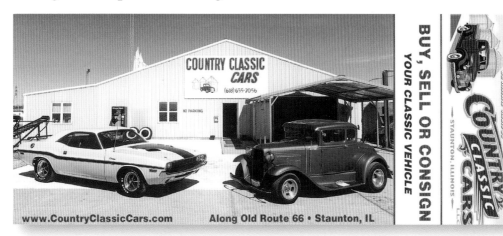

One of the largest dealers of old cars in the United States is Country Classic Cars, which we stumbled upon while driving Route 66 in Staunton, Illinois. The place always has six hundred–plus cars, and most of them are sheltered in huge barns.

Are you in the mood for a 1949 Ford sedan or a VW Squareback? Country Classic Cars can satisfy your cravings. The cars are packed as tight as sardines in the buildings, and in no particular brand order, which I liked.

I spoke to owner Russell Noel about how he became an accidental classic car dealer. "It was 1993, and my wife and I were on our way to a yard sale," he said. "On the way there, I saw an old car sitting at a man's house, so I told my wife we'd stop there after we left the yard sale."

The old car turned out to be a 1957 Chevy. The owner said he'd sell it for $500, but accepted Noel's offer of $350. Noel brought it home and did a few repairs. The car turned out to be a rare Model 150 Salesman's Coupe, which was delivered new without a rear seat.

He sold the car for $3,000.

"I told my wife that it was the easiest money I had ever made," he said. "We were just farmers. We didn't have much money, but we didn't owe any money either." So Noel started buying old cars. First it was six, then twelve, then forty. "I told my wife that if this continues, we'll get out of farming and get into old cars full-time," he said. Once that happened, though, his neighbor turned him in to the authorities for running a business out of his house. "So we bought thirteen acres along the interstate, figuring we'd have a nice, little part-time mom-and-pop operation. But that didn't last long."

These days Noel has mechanics, salesmen, and bookkeepers on staff. Country Classic Cars, which started with one 50-foot by 120-foot building, now has about a half-million square feet of indoor showroom. I can verify that the buildings are large; so large, if fact, that even if walking quickly, it takes more than an hour to tour them all.

Noel spends his days buying old cars at auctions throughout the Midwest and East Coast. He drives a four-car hauler and his brother drives a seven-car hauler. Noel said his favorite part of the business is the people that he meets. "Once Columbia Pictures came to me about renting some cars for a movie about Mohammad Ali they were filming in Chicago," he said. "They wound up renting forty-six cars and trucks from us and shipped them all up to Chicago for the production. I attend a lot of auctions. Mostly, I buy eleven cars over a weekend, but my record is twenty-one cars!

That time, my brother had to go back and pick up a second load."

Some of the cars on display were on consignment, but Noel said that he owns 90 percent of the cars at his facility outright. That is a lot of cars, even from a veteran car guy like me.

I asked Noel what kind of cars he likes to purchase. "I'm always looking for 1967 to 1969 Camaros, 1965 to 1967 Mustangs, Challengers, and Cudas," he said. "But once I bought a little Gremlin with only thirty thousand miles. A man came down from Michigan who was determined to buy the car and drive it home that day. I told him that we still didn't have the title, and that he should probably wait and have it delivered. We were asking, I think, three thousand eight hundred fifty dollars for the Gremlin, but he offered me five hundred more than we were asking just so he could drive it home that day! So we sold it to him for more money than we were asking."

Country Classic Cars keeps its less-pristine cars outside and within sight of the highway. This 1949 Ford Tudor has already been nosed and decked, stripped of chrome and Buick grille installed. Good starting point.

In closing, I asked Noel if he had any old cars of his own that he kept at home.

"Not really," he said. "I have four grandchildren, two girls and two boys. I have a 1987 Camaro IROC Z/28 convertible for each of my granddaughters, and I have a 1946 and a 1950 Chevy pickup for my grandsons." Not a bad inheritance.

MUSTANG RANCH

CAR COUNT	FOR SALE
200	★ Yes ■ No ■ Maybe

As we were approaching Missouri traveling on old Route 66, I noticed a business way off the road behind a park-and-ride lot. The sign seemed to say something about Mustangs.

Brian told me to go straight to remain on Route 66, but I veered to the left and through the park-and-ride lot. Son-of-a-gun, it was a Mustang restoration and parts business.

Tim Harville (right), his brother Shawn, and a couple of other family members are the nucleus for their business, which deals exclusively in Mustangs. Tim handles the parts counter and Shawn is the restorer.

As Michael got his camera gear out of the Explorer and Brian walked toward a lineup of old Mustangs, I walked inside to talk with the owner. I met Shawn Harville, who told me about his family's business.

"Mustang Corral has been in business for thirty-five years," he said. "I started it in 1980 when I was eighteen years old and fresh out of high school. Now I'm fifty-three and this is all I've ever done. My dad has owned Mustangs since '65, and the only cars we had when I was a kid were Mustangs."

Harville said he probably has two hundred Mustangs on the property at any one time. "We restore Mustangs for customers and we sell parts," he said. "A full restoration could take a year or two. It's primarily a family business—me, my brother, my nephew, my niece, my father. We do everything here except the paint, which we source out. We used to do painting back in the '80s, but now I just leave it to the experts."

At the time of our visit, Harville had six restorations under way, with a budget of between $50,000 and $100,000 for each one, including parts and labor. Harville said he sells both new and used parts, primarily for vintage

You want Mustangs? We got Mustangs. Tim Harville's business, Mustang Corral, is one of the original Mustang parts, restoration, and salvage businesses in the United States. It's likely that they will have any part you could need for 1964½ models until the Mustang II era.

Mustangs: "Most of the parts for newer Mustangs can be purchased on the Internet these days directly to the consumer for less money than I can buy them for, so we just concentrate on the old stuff."

He said that the most popular Mustangs were built between 1965 and 1968, when nearly two million were produced. So those are the cars he stocks the most parts for.

Harville still owns his first car, a 1973 Mustang Mach 1, which was bought new by his father. It has a 351 Cleveland with Ram-Air induction and competition suspension. "We've restored a couple of Shelbys for guys, and we had a 1965 K-Code fastback here for almost thirty years," Harville said. "We sold that just a couple of years ago."

Harville said that customers can purchase a complete project car or can pull parts off his salvage cars themselves if a similar part is not already on the shelf. He said the Internet has expanded his parts business to across the United States and even into Europe. "There are a lot of old Mustangs in Europe, and those people like old parts," he said. "Over here in America, everyone wants new parts, but in Europe, they prefer original old parts."

He has seen changes in the Mustang business since he first hung out his shingle more than three decades ago. "It seems that in the 1980s, all we were restoring were convertibles," he said. "We're here in the Midwest and the cars were so rusty—the floorpans, rockers, and torque boxes. Many of my early customers had these cars in their families for years, where the dad would pass the Mustang down to his kids. Since then we've done coupes and lately it seems we've restored more fastbacks. After the remake to *Gone in 60 Seconds*, fastbacks seemed to come out of the woodwork."

Harville said that Mustangs were the restoration "darlings" of the 1980s—everybody wanted one and there were so many around. "More were built than any other hobby car, by far," he said.

Tourists from Europe, intrigued with the Route 66 mystique, regularly walk into Harville's shop. "Here over the last ten to fifteen years, we've had a crazy amount of tourists from France, Denmark, Sweden," he said. "They love this stuff! We're like cult figures over in Europe. We've been featured in plenty of documentaries and even coffee table books."

The Mustang Corral parts inventory is large and impressive. They have more than two hundred Mustangs on the premises and buildings full of parts and sheet metal.

Just before we left Illinois, we saw this repurposed Kaiser Frazer dealership sign, which at some point in its life had become a hotel sign.

ROUTE 66

MISSOURI

E n route to the Missouri state line, we came across an original piece of Route 66 concrete pavement, probably laid down in the 1930s. It runs parallel to the current Route 66. The older road was blocked off for motor vehicle use, but we had to give it a closer inspection.

· · · · · · · ·

If this road could talk, what could it tell us about the characters that commuted on this major transcontinental artery? Did Woody Guthrie drive across this piece of pavement while he was composing "This Land Is Your Land"? Did the Barnum & Bailey Circus traverse this section of highway as it traveled from one town to another? How many families drove this highway en route to starting a new life in California?

Our mission of finding old cars paled in comparison. And as we crossed the Mississippi River and began our drive into St Louis, I realized that finding old cars in this environment would be tough. It's a city! But before we started to look for cars, Brian had a lunch date with an old coworker of his, Linda Watson Dix.

We were to meet Linda at a cool place called Mission Taco Joint on Delmar Boulevard, adjacent to the campus of Washington University in St. Louis. The food and ambiance of Mission Taco was excellent. If I didn't know we were in a Midwest city, I would have imagined I was sitting in a

Mission
TACO JOINT

"Still thinking about that delicious Chori-Huevo Torta I had @MissionTacoStl yesterday. I suggest trying one asap if you haven't yet."

-@BeerBadger08

〜〜〜

Tuesday-Saturday 11am-1am
Sunday 11am-Midnight
Closed Monday
Late Night Happy Hour 10pm-Close

THE LOOP   SOULARD
6235 Delmar Blvd   908 Lafayette Ave
314-932-5430   314-858-8226

www.missiontacojoint.com

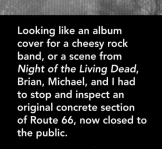

Looking like an album cover for a cheesy rock band, or a scene from *Night of the Living Dead*, Brian, Michael, and I had to stop and inspect an original concrete section of Route 66, now closed to the public.

A perfect lunch for three hard-working barn-finders.

taco restaurant in San Francisco's Mission District, where the best tacos can be found. West Coast was definitely the theme.

It was good to meet Linda and watch how she and Brian interacted after not seeing each other for many years. Back on the road, we made our way through a neighborhood and back onto Route 66. While we were sitting at a traffic light, just two blocks from where we had lunch, I looked to the right and saw an old Ford Econoline pickup. As I waited for the light to turn green, I noticed another one behind it.

MR. ECONOLINE	CAR COUNT 7	FOR SALE ☐ Yes ★ No ☐ Maybe

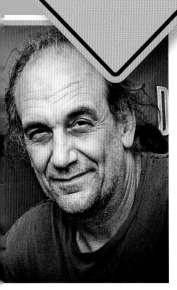

Ippolito and his brother have been buying and repairing early Econoline pickups and vans since they were teenagers.

Econoline pickups are extremely rare—I haven't seen one in years. But just two days ago, we saw one at Steve Anderson's house in Dwight, Illinois, and now here were a couple more. This was a barn-find discovery right in the heart of St. Louis!

I turned right at the next block and walked over to meet the Econoline's owner, St. Louis native, Mark Ippolito. Ippolito is a licensed electrician who uses either his early or later-model Econoline vans every day for his business. "I've been into them since I was about fifteen years old," he said. "Parts of the truck I bought when I was fifteen are still around, but the truck got smashed. Right now I'm driving an early Econoline every day. It has a 302 engine."

Ippolito has five Econoline early pickup trucks and two vans. He said the early Econoline trucks were built from 1961 through 1967, and the pickups came in both three- and five-window models.

One of the more interesting Econolines he owns features a four-wheel-drive system from a 1978 Ford truck. Ippolito is able to do most modifications on his trucks. He is an experienced welder with both MIG and TIG welders.

He also has a 1971 Mustang buried in the garage. In a serendipitous turn of events, when that Mustang was in an accident and needed a new A-pillar installed, he went to the Illinois-based Mustang Corral, where we

One of Ippolito's Econoline pickups is buried in his garage next to his Mustang. Actually a couple of more Econolines are also barricaded in the garage, where they haven't seen the light of day in quite a few years.

Ippolito is experimenting with a four-wheel-drive version of one of his Econoline vans.

had visited just that morning. They had the part and he welded it into his car. He is currently installing a 351 in one of his pickups.

I asked Ippolito if he bought and sold vintage Econolines. "I buy them and sit on them until they rust away," he said with a grin. "If I weren't married, I'd have at least three of them done. Now that I'm married, I'm in debt again."

As we were leaving Ippolito's house, we asked where we could find a real old-fashioned custard stand. "Oh, you have to go to Ted Drewes Frozen Custard," he said. He gave us directions, and we were off.

Ted Drewes could have been used in *Happy Days* or *American Graffiti*. It is an authentic custard shop and it was delicious. The specialty custard, called *concrete*, is so thick that they can turn the cup upside down to show the customer it doesn't fall out!

It ranks pretty high on this barn-find road trip team's recommendation list—see the Best-Ofs list in the back of the book for more.

We discovered that Ted Drewes is a local landmark. The store's specialty is frozen custards so thick that they can be turned upside down without spilling.

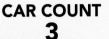

WHERE ELSE BUT 66 AUTO SALES?

CAR COUNT	FOR SALE
3	Yes ☐ No ☐ ★ Maybe

John Nieves has owned this 1955 Chevy two-door sedan for forty-five years. He has slowly been working on the body in his spare time at the dealership. He said the car brings in people off the street.

Nieves has every piece of this 1940 Ford panel. This could probably be purchased and become a very cool project for the lucky buyer.

It sounds too simple to be true, but sometimes the best place to find an old car is at a used car dealership. Case in point: We were driving along Route 66 in Pacific, Missouri, when the sight of a 1955 Chevy two-door caught my attention. It was parked at 66 Auto Sales.

We pulled our vehicles over and I noticed another couple of old vehicles. We walked around for a while and Michael took photos, but nobody was in the office. So I took the phone number from the sign and called it a few days later.

I spoke with John Nieves, seventy-five years old and ready to retire. "That's why I'm not at the dealership every day anymore," he said.

Nieves started 66 Auto Sales thirty-three years ago to sell quality used cars and play around with some of the older cars he loved. At home he has a 1964 Chevy Impala SS convertible and a 1958 Corvette. "I'd usually buy a car that needed work, restore, and sell it," Nieves said. "But I guess I would consider selling some of these older cars as-is now."

I asked him about the '55 Chevy, which is why we turned into his dealership in the first place. "I bought that one from the original old-lady owner in 1970," Nieves said. "I drove it for about ten years, then I had it in storage. I brought it to the dealership so I would have the opportunity to work on it during the day. Now there are so many people who come in to inquire about it."

Another vehicle that got our attention was a 1940 Ford Panel truck. "I bought that from a widow at an estate auction," he said. "It's not all together now, but I have every single piece for it in storage."

He also had a clean 1963 Oldsmobile Super 88. Years ago, the mother of an old friend of mine had a Super 88. I've hardly seen them since.

SHREWD CHEVY NEGOTIATOR

CAR COUNT
1

FOR SALE
☐ Yes ★ No ☐ Maybe

The sun was beginning to set when we noticed an old sedan in the parking lot of an auto repair shop. We pulled in to inquire about it and met the owner, who was there picking up his car after it had been serviced. His name was Lonnie Plunk, and he lived nearby in Villa Ridge, Missouri.

Lonnie and his wife had been searching for an old car to buy, but were becoming discouraged by the high prices people were asking, until they found this car. "This one is a 1936 Chevrolet Standard two-door sedan," Plunk said.

The biggest difference between Standard and Deluxe Chevys is that the Standard have a straight front axle, while the Deluxe models—like the 1935 on the cover of *Barn Find Road Trip*—had a knee-action suspension.

"I've had it for only three months. I went to a car show and I was walking around looking for an old car to buy. I was looking at cars that cost twenty thousand dollars, twenty-five thousand dollars. Some were fifteen thousand. Nope, too expensive for me. Then I saw this one sitting there, looked under the hood, and saw eighty-year-old grease and dirt."

Plunk noticed a "For Sale" sign sitting in the passenger seat. There was a man who was familiar to Plunk standing near the car. His name was Jason, and he runs a local restaurant.

"I asked Jason if he was thinking of buying the car, and he said no, that his wife was making him sell it," Plunk said. "Jason's wife said, 'Get it out

Just as the sun was setting, we made one more old-car contact for the day. Lonnie Plunk was just picking up his 1936 Chevy sedan from a repair shop when we met him.

of the garage. You've done nothing with it since 1981, but look at it. I want it out of here.'"

Jason told Plunk it was his dad's car; his dad bought it new. He didn't know how much he wanted to sell it for. "So I said, 'If you keep the cost down, I might be interested in buying it.' I told him I wasn't going to spend anything like fifteen thousand dollars for it," Plunk said.

Jason told him the car had appraised for $10,400. "So I said to Jason, 'So you're asking ten thousand dollars for it?' Jason said he didn't know yet. So I told him I'd see him at the restaurant. My wife and I go there about three days a week," Plunk said.

Later that week, Plunk stopped at Jason's restaurant and asked if he had sold the old Chevy yet. "Nope, nobody else even looked at it," Jason said.

"I told him that the car was just not that popular, that no museum would want to own it," Plunk said. "He understood, so I offered him five thousand dollars. He said, 'What?' But I told him that's all it was worth. I'd probably have to put another four to five thousand into it."

Plunk settled with Jason for $7,000. "It only has forty-seven thousand miles on it, about two thousand miles a year since new," Plunk said.

Plunk and his wife are as pleased as punch with their new investment. They plan to have a new interior installed and then take it to car shows and club events. Welcome, Plunks, to the world of old cars!

That night we ate and drank at Public House Brewing Company in Rolla, Missouri. Wednesday would be the start of our fourth day on the road.

◆ DAY FOUR ◆

Since leaving Chicago four days earlier, we had traveled about 550 trouble-free miles. But that wasn't guaranteed to last—we started paying attention to a major weather event that was heading toward northeast Texas, exactly where we would be traveling in the next twenty-four hours or so.

Watching the Weather Channel in the Hampton Inn breakfast area, it was hard to tell if we were actually destined to have the awful weather they were predicting or if the channel just wanted to keep people alarmed in order to keep their ratings high and their advertisers happy. The huge

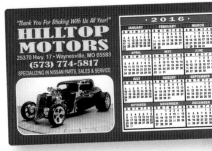

green and orange mass of clouds that were heading to Texas looked onerous enough according to the TV screen, so we decided to keep that in mind as we continued our journey south and west.

RALPH NADERMOBILES

CAR COUNT
2

FOR SALE
★ Yes   No   Maybe

Near our hotel sat a roadside souvenir shop owned by Carl and Zelma Smith that sold Route 66 memorabilia and other items. It wasn't the trinkets we were interested in, however, but the two Corvairs that were parked out front.

I'm sorry to admit that I have only just begun to truly appreciate Corvairs. I have never owned one, but my friend Bob Meade drove one in high school, so I have spent a little time behind the wheel on occasion. Lately, though, I have begun to better understand the mission of the Corvair and now realize what a bold move it was for GM to develop.

When GM virtually owned the domestic vehicle market in the late 1950s and early 1960s, the company didn't need anything besides a front-engine, rear-wheel-drive automobile to stay on the top of the sales charts. But some bold thinkers at GM decided to reinvent the automobile down to its very core.

Two cars were the result: the Corvair and the Olds Toronado. The Toronado was not only beautifully sculptured, but also driven by its front

This Corvair was parked right on the side of the highway, according to the owner, to attract attention. This four-door 1960 appears to have a very clean body and is for sale.

The 1960 Corvair has an interesting simulated grille mounted on the front. I don't know if it is a Fitch Sprint accessory or maybe a JC Whitney piece.

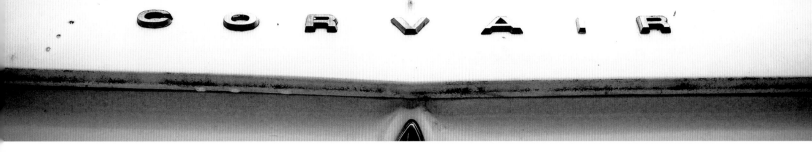

wheels during a time when only three-cylinder Saabs and the occasional Lancia were driven by their front wheels.

But the Corvair broke the GM mold even more: pancake-style rear-mounted six-cylinder engine, air-cooled, fully independent suspension, and compact in size. It's a shame the Corvair was written off to history in 1969, because with that bold thinking, who knows where GM and car design in general could have gone. More than forty-five years later, we all lament the car design and vision of the past.

Anyway, the two Corvairs in front of Zelma Smith's Mule Trading Post in Rolla, Missouri, got our attention because of how clean and original they appeared. "We've owned those cars for three or four years," said Carl Smith, who mentioned they were purchased to help draw attention to their store. "The red Corvair is a 1960 and the white one is a '64. We'd consider selling them, I suppose. We're asking $5,500 for the red one and $4,500 for the white one, and both will run with a little bit of tinkering."

DALE'S COLLECTIBLES

CAR COUNT	FOR SALE		
16	☐ Yes	☐ No	★ Maybe

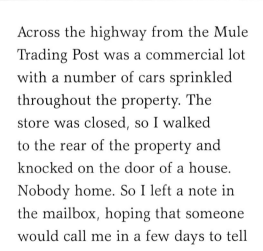

Across the highway from the Mule Trading Post was a commercial lot with a number of cars sprinkled throughout the property. The store was closed, so I walked to the rear of the property and knocked on the door of a house. Nobody home. So I left a note in the mailbox, hoping that someone would call me in a few days to tell

Something you don't see very often: a 1950 Chevy Sedan Delivery, which owner Steen said only needs a paint job.

us about their cars, then played with a puppy that was near the house as an overprotective mother dog stood watch over me.

Then we started to look around. There were Fords and Chevys and even a Baja Bug (the second one we'd found on this trip!).

A few days later, Dale Steen called me. "I've been a car dealer for forty-four years," he said as he apologized for not being home when we visited. "I was driving my granddaughter to school. I built this lot from three acres of woods. I'm a Ford guy pretty much."

Being a Ford wagon enthusiast, this '56 caught my attention, especially when I discovered it had a rare sedan delivery door with side-mounted hinges.

Virtually everything Dale had on his property was for sale except for the 1942 Ford hot rod coupe that was parked next to his house. "The '56 Ford station wagon has no engine or transmission," Steen said, "but it has a sedan delivery rear door with the hinges on the side. It was called a coroner and flower wagon, which was a special order. I'd take thirty-five hundred for that. And that little Corvair convertible that's under the shed—it has absolutely no rust. It's a four-speed car and I'd take thirty-five hundred for that as well. But it has no top."

He told me about the 1956 Ford two-door hardtop with a 351-cubic-inch and an automatic transmission that runs perfectly, which he is selling for $10,000. He also told me about two Japanese journalists who walked onto his lot a few years ago. "Neither one of them spoke any English, but they wrote a two-page story about my business that I can't read!" he said.

You know what P. T. Barnum would say—"no such thing as bad publicity." Immediately after leaving Dale Steen's collection of cars, we noticed a large salvage yard on a side road off to the right. Everywhere we looked, Rolla was a town filled with old vehicles.

Hauck found the Henry J in the backyard of the man who built and drove it decades earlier. Hauck restored the car and the original owner, now in his eighties, was the first person to drive the car again. *Joe Hauck*

As we drove to the yard, Joe Hauck, owner of Rolla Auto Wreckers, met us. Hauck told us that even though he had acres of cars, the previous owners of the yard scrapped all the older inventory before he bought it in 1985, so nearly everything that remained was late-model, 1985 and after.

"When salvage prices were high, unfortunately all the old stuff was crushed," he said. But he said he had some cars for us to look at anyway, so we followed him to his workshop for a peek.

Hauck is a racer and has made it his mission to find and resurrect old stock cars that he saw race at area dirt tracks in his youth. "This is a 1939 Willys," he said. "It's still on the Willys frame. This is just the way it looked when it was raced. My brother and I dug it out of a creek in North St. Louis three years ago. This car won championships in 1958, '61, and '62. They said I was crazy when I dragged that home. The original builder and driver is still alive and he was the first one to drive it after we restored it. It still has the original frame and back bumper, but somebody had cut off the body and took the roll cage while it was still sitting down in the creek, so we made a new body by hand. I saw this car race when I was eight or nine years old, so I had a model kit of it. I still have it, so we used that model to make the new body."

To prove his car is still in racing condition, he fired up the big-block Chevy.

Oh, what beautiful cacophony!

An early photo of the Henry J from when it was racing in the 1960s. Hauck still has a model kit of the car he built as a child. *Joe Hauck*

Hauck mentioned that he also had a vintage racing Henry J that he had also seen race as a kid, but it was not in the shop at the moment. As he walked us around his workshop, he said he used to race against local dirt-track legend Ken Schrader in the old days. Afterward, Schrader went on to race and win in the NASCAR Cup series. "Schrader still owns an old car that used to race against these cars in the old days," he said.

He showed us a 1937 Chevy stock car with a big-block and a 1966 Barracuda dirt-tracker with a slant-six engine that his daughter races. He started up another big-block so I could hear the beautiful exhaust noise of the unmuffled mill.

"That '37 has been restored since 2007, but it was originally raced in the 1950s with a six-cylinder, then a 327, then they moved up to the A class with a big-block," he said.

Hauck lives next door to the salvage yard, so he invited us over to see a 1938 Chevy coupe in his garage. He bought it when he was fifteen years old. As we walked toward the house, he told me the story about how he got interested in racing. "My dad had a salvage yard in St. Louis, but he died when I was eleven years old," he said. "When I was ten, he taught me how to weld on that old '37 Chevy I just showed you."

As he opened the garage door at his house, he told us about how he came to acquire the coupe. "I bought it for two hundred dollars when I was fifteen from a guy who owned the winery in St. James," he said. "I put a six-volt battery in it and drove it home. The original engine was a

Hauck bought this 1938 Chevy coupe when he was a teenager with the intention of cutting it up into stock car. Thank goodness that never happened and he built it into a street rod instead. He is getting ready to rebuild it again.

six-cylinder, but that's long gone. I came close to chopping it up for a race car—you know, the things you do when you are fifteen. Now I'm glad I didn't. I found another car to use as a race car just about the time I was getting ready to start cutting this one apart."

The car is solid, but definitely an old-school hot rod. Today, it has a small-block Chevy and a five-speed transmission, "anything to get it down the road," he said. "It's hard to drive with the dropped front axle. I built it in 1975; that's when I learned how to paint."

It also has the largest set of rear fender flares I've seen in a long time. Hauck, his brother, and stepfather fabricated them from flat steel. He said he was thinking of widening the entire fender and narrowing the flare when he does the car over. "It had wide Mickey Thompsons on it when I built it, but those tires are long gone," he said.

He then showed us photos of his Henry J race car, when it was raced back in the day, and now. The Henry J was beautiful. "It was built back in the sixties," Hauck said. The driver raced in NASCAR the first year Daytona opened.

"Then it sat behind the owner's barn for forty-nine years before I bought it. He figured out a long time ago about how to work with the wind and aerodynamics, way before anyone else. He just turned eighty-seven years old last month."

The Henry J had a large scoop on each side. I asked Hauck about those. "The builder was hung up with the 1950s Corvettes, so he built that feature into seven of his race cars. It runs today with a 429 Ford. It actually ran with a 427 back in the 1960s, but I didn't think I'd ever find one of those."

Joe Hauck and his brothers Kurt (now deceased) and Henry—who did all the hand lettering on the race cars—were amazing craftsmen. I know that if I am in the Rolla area during the Gateway Vintage Racing Association season, I will go out of my way to see these cars turn laps.

A rusty, crusty Ford panel truck body caught our attention. Then we saw that the building next to it seemed to have a hot rod theme. So we parked the Woody and walked inside.

Two workmen, who were pushing around garbage with a Bobcat, explained what was happening. "The business that was in here was called Hot Rod City," one of them said. The sign against the building said it was a Do-It-Yourself Hot Rod Shop, but I couldn't figure out what that meant.

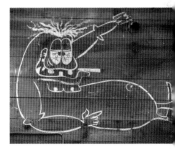

The story he told us about the building, though, was even more intriguing.

"This building was built as a roller skating rink by singer Charlie Rich when he was stationed in the army at [nearby] Fort Leonard Wood," he said. "The crazy artwork on the walls was hand-painted in 1960."

It was very reminiscent of the Big Daddy Ed Roth style of monster art. He said the guy who owned the hot rod business here went bankrupt, so they were hired to clean up the building and install a new roof so that it could be rented to a new tenant. Hopefully that new tenant will leave the cool artwork in place.

◆ STEP BACK IN TIME ◆

Because I had recently returned from a car-hunting trip to Cuba, I saw a few similarities between Cuba and the towns we passed through on Route 66.

Both the towns along Route 66 and the country of Cuba were once beautiful and flamboyant, but now much of that past glory is spoiled. Both Cuba and the towns along Route 66 probably peaked at about the same time, in the late 1950s.

Driving on Route 66 is truly a step back in time. The buildings, hotels, gas stations, houses, and stores are from a time before interstate highways.

Some of those buildings are well maintained, some not so much, and some are completely ramshackle and tumbling down.

Like so many people who yearn to see Cuba in its raw state before it becomes modernized, I highly recommend a Route 66 adventure before it changes or further deteriorates. One more interesting note: there is a Cuba in Missouri. The City of Cuba, right on Route 66, is known as the City of Murals. As many towns on the old route have fought to survive since the interstate highway system was installed—erecting Route 66 museums, etc.—Cuba chose a mural theme to make the town memorable. As we drove through Cuba, we were impressed with the size and the quality of the artwork.

◆ ON THE ROAD AGAIN . . . ◆

In St. Roberts, we noticed a showroom full of old vehicles. The sign on the window said "Ozark Classic Cars." The doors were locked, so we peeked

HISTORY OF A CLASSIC

The song "Route 66," originally titled "Get Your Kicks on Route 66," was written in 1946 by American songwriter Bobby Troup. The song's lyrics were a tribute to the path that Federal Highway 66 took through two-thirds of the country from Chicago to LA.

Nat King Cole of the Nat King Cole Trio first sang the song in 1946. It became a hit and rose to prominence on *Billboard Magazine*'s R&B and pop charts. Bing Crosby, Chuck Berry, The Rolling Stones, and Asleep at the Wheel all later performed the song.

The idea for the song came to Troup during a cross-country drive from Pennsylvania to California. Troup wanted to try his hand as a Hollywood songwriter, so he and his wife, Cynthia, packed up their 1941 Buick and headed west. The trip began on Highway 40 and continued along Route 66 to the California coast. Troup initially considered writing a tune about Highway 40, but Cynthia suggested the title "Get Your Kicks on Route 66." The song was composed on the ten-day journey and completed by referencing maps when the couple arrived in Los Angeles.

THE ELBOW INN

In Devil's Elbow, Missouri, we visited a well-known Route 66 landmark, the Elbow Inn. Known for its barbecue sandwiches and dinners, it is equally famous for all the bras tacked to the ceiling!

The tradition at the Elbow Inn is a "shot for a shot." Women are challenged to remove their bras and give the bartender a "shot," or a glance, in exchange for a free shot of whiskey from the bar.

The Elbow Inn was built in the 1920s as the Munger Moss Sandwich Shop and was later turned into apartments before it reverted into a barbecue shack.

World Famous
THE ELBOW INN
— ESTABLISHED 1929 —

MISSOURI
U S
66

"Most Historic Bar & Restaurant On Route 66"
Great Fun • Great Food • Great Prices
Only 2 Minutes From St. Robert

(573) 336-5375
21050 Teardrop Road • Devils Elbow, MO 65457
Facebook - ELBOW INN BAR & BBQ

Our Friendly Staff

Historic Route 66 Devil's Elbow Bridge, Devils Elbow Missouri

into the large windows. We noticed at least two dozen 1940s to 1960s Ford and Chevy convertibles. This was a fabulous collection that appeared to be forgotten. Thankfully there were large windows, so at least people could peer in as opposed to the vehicles being trapped inside a windowless warehouse.

There was no phone number on display, so we just kept driving down the road.

Later, we discovered that the local businessman who owned those cars had died and left the collection to his daughter, who lived out of town. She has no intention of selling anything, so they just sit as a free roadside attraction for tourists to stop and photograph through the showroom windows.

MAJESTIC HOT ROD BUILDER/ COLLECTOR

CAR COUNT	FOR SALE		
7 (23)	☐ Yes	★ No	☐ Maybe

York was once a guitarist for country music star Narvel Felts. Felts had forty-one hits before cutting off his finger working on a hot rod. The guitar is a 1964 Fender Stratocaster.

We drove past a place just up the street from Ozark Classic Cars called Majestic Auto Body in the town St. Roberts. I noticed an old Chevy truck peeking out of the garage door, then spied a '57 Chevy. By the time we pulled into the parking lot, I could see several old vehicles, all in primo condition.

I walked in and met lifelong hot rodder and owner, Ken York. "I've been building hot rods for sixty-eight years," he said. "We build everything right here—paint, fabrication, everything."

I asked York which car he has owned the longest. He pointed to a black 1955 Chevy two-door hardtop. "I've owned that one since 1958," he said. "I graduated from high school in 1959. That was my first car. I paid under five hundred dollars for it. It had nine hundred miles on the odometer."

York showed me photos of himself with the Chevy, including one of him washing the car when he was seventeen years old and another driving the car to his senior prom.

Ken York bought this 1955 Chevy as a high school junior in 1958. Besides an engine swap and pinstriping, the car is largely original down to its never-used spare tire.

Early in his ownership, York removed the original 265-cubic-inch engine and installed a 283. He also installed a Corvette tri-power carb setup in 1959. The Chevy still retains a three-on-the-tree standard transmission. "The only modifications I really did to this car was paint pinstripes on the body and the dashboard," he said. "I painted those pinstripes myself in 1960." York opened the Chevy's trunk and proudly showed us the car's never-used spare tire. The car now has 80,000 miles.

I counted two 1955 Chevys in the garage and one 1957, all two-door hardtops. We walked over to the other '55, which was orange and white. York told me he painted that car

The very same car when York was washing it soon after purchasing it. For a man who is a lifelong hot rodder, it's amazing that he never modified this car.
Ken York

Before this '57 Chevy was restored as a street car, it was York's drag car. Since then it has received a flamed paint job, Buick grille, and a show finish on the chassis and floorpans.

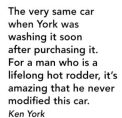

in lacquer thirty-seven years ago. The car still has its original interior as well as the original 265 engine and four-barrel carb. "That '57 was my drag race car," he said. "Then I converted it back to a street-legal car. It has a L82 Corvette engine. You need to go and look underneath this car," he continued. "The chassis and the floors shine as nice as the body."

I got on my knees and took a peek. The man wasn't lying!

Even though York is a self-proclaimed Chevy man, he owns a pristine 1965 MGB. As we were preparing to say goodbye, York mentioned that he also owns a 1965 Impala with a 409 engine and a 1950 Mercury.

"You have more cars than this?" I asked.

"I own twenty-three altogether, all in the same condition as these."

SCRAP METAL AND ZS	CAR COUNT 775	FOR SALE ★ Yes No Maybe

We soon passed what appeared to be an overgrown scrapyard not far from Ken York's garage. There were cars piled high in every direction, fighting the foliage for space.

I walked through a narrow path between piles of aluminum scrap and junk cars to a building, and that's where I met Richard Jensen. Jensen told me he is both a scrap metal dealer and a Datsun/Nissan parts dealer. "I've got about seventy-five Datsuns here, mostly Zs, and about seven hundred more on my farm, about fifteen miles away," he said.

Seven hundred seventy-five Datsuns! That's a serious collection. That includes 510s, 610s, roadsters, etc. He's got them all. "I sell between fifteen and twenty-five a year," he said. "Just enough to pay the bills. I took over this business in 1988. People find out about me through word of mouth. I sell Datsun and Nissan 240, 260, 280, and 300 Z-cars and parts all around the country."

I asked if he has a favorite old car. He said *yes* and walked us through the brush and showed us a Willys Jeep wagon that he parked under a shed

Richard Jensen, who besides Z-cars, collects scrap metals and aluminum, knows where every piece and part is located in his very crowded yard.

The best sign! Richard Jensen does no advertising and relies on word-of-mouth references for people to find his Datsun Z-car salvage yard. Of course this orange Z-car elevated over the freeway doesn't hurt either . . .

roof in 1988. "I guess I'll restore this when I retire," Jensen mused. "My wife drives a 1993 Z-car, but I never have personally cared much about them because they rust out too fast."

DADDY'S OLD GARAGE

CAR COUNT	FOR SALE		
61	☐ Yes	☐ No	★ Maybe

"Our daddy ran this place since 1946, and our grandpa owned a Shell Station across the highway staring in 1929," said Bill Jones Jr. "I saw the 66 Highway come through here when I was six years old in 1956."

Brothers Bill and Roger Jones have been around cars and Bill's Garage in Lebanon, Missouri, their whole lives. They used to live in the Shell station until the highway made them tear it down in 1956. "Part of the old building was moved right over there," Roger said as he pointed to a roof and a chimney next door.

"I remember as a kid, going with my dad to haul in cars when people would break down on the highway," Bill Jr. said. "Dad was really the only garage in the area."

Bill (left) and Roger Jones are the third generation of mechanics and car tinkerers on this property. Their grandfather had a service station and their father Bill Sr. rescued stranded motorists along Route 66 for decades.

The old Bill's Garage is now operated on a part-time basis by Bill's sons, Bill and Roger Jones. Around the property are dozens of interesting old vehicles, such as this 1955 Chevy Sedan Delivery.

A rare and ideal starting point for a unique hot rod project, a 1936 Dodge panel truck, identifiable because of the "hump" in the roofline, which differentiates it from Chevys and Fords of the era.

Excuse me if I feature a number of Nashes in this book, but I truly have fallen in love with the 1950s art-deco designs of the brand. This one is crying out for attention. It sits in the side yard of Bill's Garage.

Bill Jr. was into Novas and Roger was mostly a Chevelle fan.

"Everybody builds V-8s, but I like those six-cylinder Novas," Bill Jr. said.

As I scanned their property, I saw a number of Chevelles and Novas, as well as a selection of other cars. I counted sixty-one old cars, to be exact. A random sampling included 1955 and 1957 Chevy sedan deliveries, a 1938 Ford gas tank truck, a 1950 Nash, a 1956 Hudson, a 1956 Studebaker station wagon, and an odd homemade T-bucket-type creation with a VW torsion bar front suspension and a big-block Chevy engine.

"We never really closed the business," Bill Jr. said. "I worked here for many years, then left to go to work at a dealership downtown. But we've always piddled with this stuff [old cars], so we're still open. People come knock on the door every day. Everyone wants to buy these old cars."

Answering the question that nobody asked . . . brothers Bill and Roger are quick to point out that they did not build this big-block, VW torsion-bar suspended, homemade steel replica of a '23 T-bucket.

"We love meeting all the people from other countries. Lots of times, only one of them can speak English, so he's the interpreter for the rest of them. They'll take pictures of the cars, have a picnic, whatever," Bill Jr. adds. "Once, a British car club had the whole driveway filled with Triumphs and MGs," added Roger, who lives in the adjacent house. "About fifteen of them."

"Another group of European tourists came through with a bunch of mopeds," Bill Jr. said. "They were a moped club from Europe and they had their bikes shipped over to Chicago. I think they only made about thirty miles a day. We just enjoy meeting all the people."

The sun was setting and we were reaching that "magic light" time of day, according to Michael. We were hoping to haul tail through the countryside along Route 66 to try to make it to our hotel in Joplin, Missouri, before it got too dark. But, as you can imagine, our progress was slowed when we saw an old Studebaker in a farm field, surrounded by a couple of other cars. We just had to stop.

STUDEBAKER EDUCATOR

CAR COUNT	FOR SALE		
5	☐ Yes	★ No	☐ Maybe

We drove up the driveway and knocked on the door of the house. We met a wonderful guy named Keith Marlin. We asked about the Studebaker, and he told us its tale.

"A friend of mine was going through a divorce, so he asked me to keep this car for him," Marlin said, referring to the 1956 Golden Hawk. "That was in 1987, and I'm still holding the car. I've had it so long now that I think I'll just go ahead and restore it. It still has a pretty sound body. My friend is fifteen, twenty years older than me, so I'm sure he won't mind if I take it for myself after all these years."

Keith Marlin is a typical car guy, just like all the rest of us: too many projects and not enough time! The college professor hopes to retire soon and jump on some of his stillborn restorations.

Marlin also has this 1954 Studebaker, which is not as solid as the '56. He hopes to hot rod it with a Chevy drivetrain.

Marlin's first car. He purchased this 1957 Chevy two-door in 1970. It's a shame this car is sitting outside, deteriorating. Before leaving, I encouraged Marlin to get it in a garage before it becomes impractical to restore.

While we were talking to Marlin, the sky was growing dark—a result of the impending storm we had been tracking since the beginning of our trip. The sun and clouds were painting a different watercolor in the sky about every minute. Michael was getting anxious to shoot.

But back to the car. "Most of the Studebakers have a 289, but this Golden Hawk has 352 Packard motor," Marlin said. "When I stored this car for my friend, I got bit by the Studebaker bug and started to learn more about them."

He pointed to another Studebaker in the corner of the field, a 1954. Marlin said he would like to hot rod that one. He said he would probably install a Chevy drivetrain because of parts availability.

I asked Marlin about the 1957 Chevy two-door that was sitting in the field. "That was my first car," he said. "I bought it in 1970, I think it was. It was a six-cylinder, but my brother and I converted it to a 327 and a four-speed. It was my hot rod back in the day."

I asked him why such a prized car as a 1957 Chevy was deteriorating out in a field. He answered, and I completely understood.

"I've had three kids and I put them through college," he said. "I never wanted to sacrifice that. These days I teach college psychology, but I was a high school counselor for over twenty-five years."

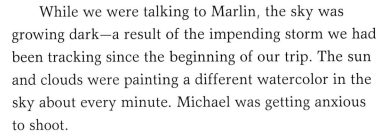

The car that made us stop one more time en route to our hotel as the sun was setting. Keith Marlin has been storing this 1956 Studebaker Golden Hawk for a friend for decades. Now Marlin says he is going to restore it for himself.

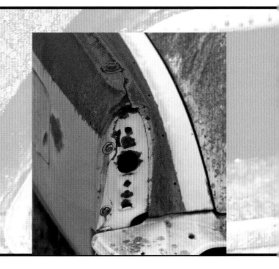

A Studebaker tutorial—Keith Marlin educated us on the difference between a Studebaker Golden Hawk and a Silver Hawk. The higher-level Golden Hawk (left) has a fiberglass fin extension that bolts on top of each rear quarter panel. The Silver Hawk has the same quarter panel, but without the fiberglass extension, as on the example on the right.

He said the Chevy will need floorpans when he finally restores it. "My youngest daughter is a senior in high school now, so there's light at the end of the tunnel," he laughed.

Day four was quickly coming to an end. It had been a good one—we'd found a bunch of interesting cars and met some amazing people.

We made it to Joplin for the evening. We were booked at a La Quinta hotel, which was an odd restoration of an older property. But we had a good night's sleep and were eager to hit the road again first thing in the morning.

◆ DAY FIVE, JOPLIN, MISSOURI ◆

We woke up and walked what seemed like a mile to the free breakfast bar. Man, that was a long hallway.

After breakfast, Brian and Michael were still loading the Ford Explorer as I fired up the Woody, waiting near the hotel parking lot exit. As I waited, a man named Chuck Comer emerged from the Starbucks coffee shop next door with his morning coffee. He saw my Woody and drove his pickup truck over to the La Quinta to have a closer look.

"Nice car," he said. I thanked him. On this trip, I had been hearing a lot of "nice car."

He told me he had some parts for a 1940 Ford Woody, a virtually *identical* car to my 1939. Comer had my attention. He gave me his business card and it featured a 1940 Willys coupe that he said he owned from the 1970s. This guy was the real deal.

I told him we were driving Route 66 looking for old cars. He said we could follow him to his business—a towing yard a few miles away—because he had a couple of vehicles we might be interested in.

It was quite a fortuitous meeting.

HOT FOR HOT RODS AND THE RACE CAR GRAVEYARD

CAR COUNT	FOR SALE
50+	Yes No ★ Maybe

Chuck Comer, the man in Joplin, Missouri, who has his hand on the pulse of hot rodding! Chuck's towing yard doubles as his private barn-find museum for vintage tin, old hot rods, and race cars.

Chuck Comer is a hot rodder's hot rodder. He has worked hard building his towing business, but has also worked hard to collect and restore some amazing hot rods and race cars. As we walked into the storage yard (where he stores wrecked cars until the insurance companies decide their fates), I passed relic after relic, car after car.

"There's a '56 Chevy, and there's an old dirt track car, a '59 Chevy, a '61 Chevy," I said to no one in particular as I rambled through the lot.

"See that '39 Ford there?" asked Comer. "That was my dad's car. He just stopped driving it one day. He said it had fender skirts on the rear and it was raised up in the front. But it's been sitting for fifty years. It was hot rodded the way they did it back then." Comer said the car was still restorable, that the floors and body were basically solid, but that he can only do so many cars at a time.

In the weeds behind the '39 Tudor were a couple of sprint cars on trailers. "And there are a couple of '55 Chevys back there, but you'd have to climb back there through the 'Jesus' thorns that

Partially hidden by weeds, this 1956 Chevy wagon is typical of the many cars in Comer's yard. Behind this wagon were literally dozens of old race cars hidden in the tall brush.

When I met Comer in the hotel parking lot, he showed me a photo of his 1940 Willys gasser coupe. Little did I know that he had several others, including this 1939 Willys sedan, which could become a heck of a project for some lucky rodder.

Under a shed roof, Comer had this 1940 Ford Deluxe Coupe. It was an extremely solid car from Nebraska. By keeping his eyes open, he has found many cars like this in his hometown of Joplin.

are about that long—"showing us a three-inch spike with his fingers—"and they'll get you."

Comer walked us deeper into his lot. We came upon a belly-tank Bonneville racer that was powered by a rear-mounted V-8 60 Ford flathead. Behind the belly-tank was a 1939 Willys sedan. Comer told me there was another one behind it in the weeds. "Here's a 1956 Chevy wagon . . . there's a 1957 Chevy wagon . . ." Thinking out loud again. This was clearly a barn-finder's goldmine.

Comer had owned some of these cars for so long—thirty to forty years—he couldn't remember where he got them. He has been in the towing business (Chuck's Towing) for thirty-five years. He currently has six rigs on the road. He said that sometimes he lucks into unique old cars when a customer calls to have them removed from their yard, but mostly he searches and keeps his ears open, the same way we do.

We walked past a mid-1930s-era Ford panel truck. There was another one. And another one. And Chuck told us there were a few more in the weeds. "Most of my good cars are at home," he said. "And in the storage buildings next door. There are some Corvettes, some 1940 Fords."

A row of old dirt track racers was along the fence line, mostly hidden by weeds. "These used to race here in town when I was a kid," he said. "Some I've bought, some were dropped off by people who know I collect this stuff. Others I've bought for the scrap value before they went to the

Comer's first car, a 1955 Chevy two-door wagon, which he drove to high school, raced, and used to date young ladies.

crusher. There are still a couple of old race cars out there that I'd like to have, but the old guys won't sell them. Like a nice Model A in Tulsa that looks like a sprint car. The old guy won't sell it to me, but I'll get it one day, if I outlive him," he said with a chuckle.

I asked Comer about the Willys coupe on his business card. It was prepared in the gasser style, and I've always had a warm spot in my heart for Willys gassers, especially the Stone, Woods & Cook car. "I bought it back in about 1977 when a couple of guys and I were looking for old cars," he said. "We found this one locally, but my friends wanted to part it out; this guy wanted the trunk lid, that guy wanted the fenders. I said, 'I think I want to fix that one up,' so I gave the owner one hundred fifty dollars for it. I was just a kid." He said it had been an old drag car when he bought it, partially disassembled, no engine, but traction bars were mounted.

This altered wheelbase Dodge Dart street/ drag car was too good for Comer to pass up. When Comer finishes projects like this, he either stores them in his adjacent storage building or brings them home.

As we walked from the back toward the front of the property, we passed other random vehicles, like an odd altered-wheelbase Dodge Dart with a huge hood scoop, 440 engine, and a four-speed. "A local fellow built that car, and it was kind of crude, so when he was getting ready to sell it; I bought it," Comer said.

He walked us toward a carport area where several cars were under roof. One vehicle that immediately caught my eye was an early Cabover flatbed truck. "It's a 1946 General Motors Cabover that sits on a motorhome

chassis," he said. "It has a Chevy 454 sitting below the sleeper cab. After 1946, they changed the name to GMC, but this was still a General Motors."

On the back of the flatbed was an amazing 1934 Ford three-window coupe. "That one is right out of the fifties," he said. "It's just an old flathead-powered fifties hot rod. I have a picture of it on the drag strip back then."

Next to the Cabover sat a 1955 Chevy two-door wagon. "That was my first car," Comer said. "I paid one hundred twenty-five dollars for it. I took it to my parents' house and my dad yelled at me for wasting so much money on it."

Next to the two-door was a 1940 Ford coupe that Comer found on the way to dropping off scrap one day. The owner had just moved from Nebraska and wanted to sell it, so Comer was happy to take it off his hands.

He showed us a ¾-ton early-forties-era Ford panel truck that he would like to sell for $2,500.

As we were preparing to leave, Comer opened up a steel building and revealed an honest-to-God Jeff Gordon, No. 24 DuPont NASCAR Cup Chevy Lumina car. He said he bought it from a gentleman in Charlotte down the street from Hendrick Motorsports, right near where Brian and I live. Next to that was an ex–Tony Bettenhausen midget racer currently powered by a V-8 60.

And more coupes and more sedan deliveries, and more race cars . . .

Sometimes I think I'm living the dream. Chuck Comer is *also* living the dream. This was an amazing morning, and it illustrates just how valuable driving an interesting old car can be while hunting for barn-finds. Had we not been driving the Woody, nor had perfect timing before and after that *long*

HONK AS YOU PASS

The hardest thing about a barn-find road trip is passing by so many old cars without stopping. Even though we are searching for old cars on Route 66, we also have a two-week deadline to complete the drive from Chicago to the Santa Monica pier. So it's a constant struggle of documenting cars versus getting to LA on time.

Sometimes there is a terrific old car that we just don't have time to inspect. But as we pass by, we say a little Hail Mary, hoping that future barn-finders should be so lucky.

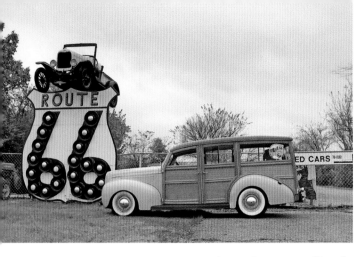

The huge sign that dragged us off Route 66 and into Don Green's "hobby business." Green is a lifelong hot rodder and drag racer who sold his scrap business years ago and now concentrates on restoring his many old cars.

walk to the breakfast buffet before checking out of the hotel that morning, we never would have met Chuck Comer.

When we left Chuck's shop in Joplin, we were less than 20 miles from the Kansas state line. We decided to just sprint toward the border and notch another state on our belt. So as we drove down Route 66, passing through a part of town that was heavily populated with late-model salvage yards, another car on the left caught my attention.

Not only that, but there was a huge Route 66 sign that would be perfect to photograph the Woody next to. So we turned around and doubled back.

CHICKEN COOP CUSTOM CADDY

CAR COUNT	FOR SALE
30	★ Yes ☐ No ☐ Maybe

At ninety years old, Green has not slowed down. He still goes to auctions, builds hot rods, and restores old cars. He has the energy and enthusiasm of a twenty-five-year-old.

As Michael photographed the sign, Brian and I inspected the rusty convertible. We couldn't tell what brand it was—some kind of British convertible with a flathead V-8 resting in the engine bay. We walked further back and saw more old cars. We couldn't just pass this place up; there was a story here.

A couple hundred feet from the road was a beguiling old-time village with a bunch of vintage cars sprinkled around.

Intriguing.

I went off to find the owner while Michael and Brian inspected the cars and shot some photographs. I walked into a building and met the owner, Don Green, a ninety-year-old hot rodder and owner of M&M Used Cars. "I've been in business here since 1960, but I've been a hot rodder my whole life," he said. "I used to do auto salvage, but I don't do that anymore. At one time we had forty two hundred cars on this property. I sold out when scrap metal was selling for a lot of money. Since I retired in 1985, I just work on old cars. These days I sell old cars, buy old cars, and fix old cars."

Green built a simulated "village" where he parks a row of old cars to delight tourists. He once had more than four thousand cars on the property, but these days only keeps a few dozen old cars of all types.

Green started to list some of the cars he had in storage buildings and at his house. They included a selection of Model T Fords from 1910 and later; some restored Cadillacs; two Model A roadsters, a 1929 and a 1931; a '32 Ford roadster; a '34 Ford roadster; a '36 Ford roadster; and a '32 Chevy coupe, just for starters. "Some of them I have in my house; others are in buildings around the property," he said.

Since Green was a hot rodder, I asked if he had ever raced. "Yes, I used to drag race a B-Gas 1932 Chevy," he said. "It had a straight front axle and I ran both fuel-injected small-block and big-block Chevys. It ran in the nines."

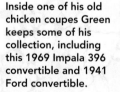

We walked toward a former chicken coop where he stored a few cars. "Here's a '64 Chevelle convertible that I restored with a big-block," Green said. "And over there is a car you've never seen: a 1959 Cadillac Fleetwood four-door convertible. That's because they never made one. But the electric top works great, goes up and down without a problem. I modified an Oldsmobile convertible top to work by adding about four inches to it."

Inside one of his old chicken coupes Green keeps some of his collection, including this 1969 Impala 396 convertible and 1941 Ford convertible.

He uncovered a couple of Model As, a 1941 Ford convertible, a purple 1934 Ford with a Corvette engine, and a 1969 Chevy Impala 396 convertible that runs well. "It sat in a garage for twenty years before I bought it," he said. "I'd take five thousand dollars for it."

He also has a solid old MGB roadster, probably a pre-1967. He said he'd take $900 for it. Don Green is an amazing car guy who has not slowed down, even at ninety years old. I'm so glad we stopped and met him.

We were done with Missouri—it was a great state to hunt for old cars. Kansas awaits!

ROUTE 66

KANSAS

T he storm we had been tracking all week looked huge and threatening. It was heading north out of southwestern Texas and toward Oklahoma and Kansas—exactly where we were heading.

· · · · · · · ·

I don't know much about weather systems—certainly nothing about the severe storms that frequent the flatlands of the Midwest. But as we drove from sunny and clear Missouri toward the distant threatening skies of Kansas, the increasing dark certainly got our attention. Could the Woody make it through?

I had a strange daydream about driving the Woody into a tornado and the birdseye maple body coming apart in splinters. But in the dream Brian and I remained on Route 66, driving a bare chassis, looking for old cars.

"Hey Brian, look, there's a '56 Studebaker pickup blowing over the top of us," I imagined saying as I wrestled to keep the rapidly deteriorating Woody on the road.

The sky turned the color of a bruise, dark and ominous. A few scattered raindrops pitter-pattered on the roof, but that distraction turned into a deluge. As luck would have it, we had just passed a Walmart shopping center, so we made a U-turn and pulled into the parking lot. You can't mess with Mother Nature while driving an American classic.

Webster
Res.

Hays

Cedar Bluff
Res.

KANSAS

Great

dge City

Historic
BYWAY

KANSAS
US

66

Check out the skies we were driving through. We were finally meeting the weather system we had been tracking for several days.

With all due respect to Judy Garland, "Toto, I don't know if we are in Kansas anymore . . ."

En route to Coffeyville, Kansas, we came across this 1937 Ford coupe that was for sale on the side of the road. This photo has perfect composition, with the green grass, the coupe, and the stormy sky.

It was absolutely pouring, so Brian, Mike, and I did what any hearty American males would do at a potentially stressful time like this—we reclined our seats and took a nap.

The heavy rain on the canvas top was like a sleeping pill. I've been told the best place to sleep during a rainstorm is in a tin-roof tobacco shed, but now I have to disagree. The Woody proved to be a perfect alternative to the shed. When we woke up an hour later, the rain was over and the sun was peeking out. (Amazingly, the one hour of rain we had just experienced would be the only precipitation we would experience after more than three weeks on the road!)

We were back on the road again and didn't lose too much time in our journey.

Of the eight states on our 2,000-plus-mile Route 66 journey, only 13 of those miles meander through Kansas. The pie-shaped wedge on our map through the Sunflower State would only take about twenty minutes to drive through.

This presented us with a potential dilemma; when my publisher Zack Miller and I discussed how we should "construct" this book, we decided that each state should be its own chapter. For states such as Illinois or Missouri, which we had just passed through, the many miles produced many barn-finds, and therefore "healthy" chapters. But how could I write a healthy chapter with only 13 miles? What if we didn't find any cars? .

In order to cover ourselves, we asked for leads on barn-finds from some of the people we had spoken with over the previous couple of days. Chuck Comer, the hot rodder from Joplin, Missouri, suggested we look for an auto salvage yard near Coffeyville, Kansas. "It's one of the last old-car junkyards left," Comer told us. We decided that even though Coffeyville was more than a stone's throw from Route 66, it promised to provide material for the healthy chapter that you deserve.

RACETRACK SALVAGE OFF THE BEATEN PATH

CAR COUNT	FOR SALE
2,500	★ Yes ☐ No ☐ Maybe

Brian Googled "Purkey's Auto Salvage" and entered the address into his phone's map program. But the GPS guided us to a dirt road in the middle of farmland—not a rust bucket to be seen.

Maybe this was where Purkey's *was* and not necessarily where it *is*. But Comer was so confident that we would be pleased with the extensive collection that we decided to call and see if Purkey's was still in business.

A woman answered the phone. "No, you can't trust the GPS directions to find us," she said, "or else you'll wind up in the middle of a farm field."

She told us to go back into the town of Coffeyville and follow her directions. We did, and again we were on a dirt road. Because it had just rained buckets, the road was wet, but the high rock content of the surface made it bearable to drive on.

Both Brian and I worked in professional auto racing for many years, so we instantly noticed the grandstands in the heavily treed distance. A racetrack? We didn't know anything about a racetrack.

As we approached the grandstand, it appeared that Purkey's Auto Salvage and the racetrack were somehow connected. We walked into the office and met the woman who had given us the directions we needed. Her name was Wanda Purkey.

I gave her a quick explanation of our intention—driving Route 66 looking for old cars for a book—and asked if we could tour and photograph her salvage yard.

"Sure, but remember, we close at five p.m.," she said.

I reasoned that wouldn't be a problem, because it was only 1:30 p.m. "We'll probably be out of here in an hour," I said as we walked out the office door and into what appeared to be a small junkyard.

You want 1959 Chevys? Purkey's Auto Salvage has some. Dozens of them, in fact, all neatly lined up. Behind those '59s was a row of 1958 Chevys, and so forth.

Famous last words, I thought. Boy, was I wrong. I had seen a few old cars behind the office and garage building, which was elevated over the adjoining area. What I didn't see was all the property that was downhill, out of sight and behind the trees.

This place was huge.

Rather than list the cars we found, like in some of the other stories in this book, I'll just give a general overview from 30,000 feet. We didn't find one '58 or '59 Chevy, but rows and rows and rows of them. And 1960 Chevys, and '57 Fords, and '53 Pontiacs, and so forth.

Here's a row of Oldsmobiles. Other rows of cars are dedicated to Pontiacs, Ramblers, Fords, Corvairs, and on and on. The late Bud Purkey, who founded the yard, did an amazing job of keeping cars in brand and year order.

This yard was so well organized that there were "territories" set up by brands. We walked through acres of Fords, neatly arranged by year and model. The same thing for Mopars, American Motors products, etc. It was jaw-dropping.

Once our eyes had seen the light, we were in no hurry to leave and return to the road. This was the kind of salvage yard my father and I used to frequent on Long Island and in New England when I was a kid. Purkey's was worthy of a book or a video documentary in and of itself!

What amazed me most was the fact that these cars were nearly complete. I'm used to walking into vintage yards and seeing rusted and stripped hulks. But Purkey's was populated with cars that mostly still retained grilles, bumpers, taillights, windows, dash gauges, and more. We saw a few cars that appeared to be 100 percent complete, capable of starting up and driving out.

Because Bud Purkey was a racer, and he had the land, he built a dirt track on his property in the early nineties. The family promoted races there until Bud got too ill to manage it.

After coming back into the office, muddy and tired, I interviewed Wanda and her son, Al Purkey, about the business. Wanda is the widow of Bud Purkey, who passed away in 2008. "Bud opened the yard in 1969," she said. "There was nothing here, just hedge trees, rocks, and cactus. The ground here is not good enough for farming—too many rocks. We bought about sixty acres and all of it is used for the cars except for a little five-acre section where I keep my cows."

Wanda told us that Bud was also a racer and that he decided to build a dirt track on the property. "We raced there until he got sick, about ten years ago," she said. She said it was called Stateline Speedway.

"Stateline"—I had to ask Wanda if we were indeed still in Kansas. I had no idea!

"Yes, you're standing in Kansas," she smiled. "Oklahoma is across the street."

Whew! I got nervous for a second that we would not be able to use Purkey's in our Kansas chapter unless we found a way to bend time and space.

We spoke about Route 66 for a couple of minutes before getting back into the conversation of old cars. Wanda was curious about the current status of the historic highway we had just passed through and wanted to hear about the old towns on it. I told her some of the towns we passed were vibrant while others were extremely depressed.

"Yes, when the interstate highways bypass these towns, then the town is basically dead," she confirmed. Wanda told us that because they had been in business for so many years, it was still a viable enterprise, but it wasn't like the old days. "The salvage business is not what it used to be because of the influx of aftermarket parts," she said. "Plus, cars are lasting a lot longer these days."

I asked if she owned an old car that might have been her husband's.

"No, but I have some of his old race cars," she said. "He raced on dirt and his last race car was a late-model. He started to race probably in 1966 when we had a small yard in south Coffeyville. We opened the racetrack in 1991. Our weekly shows weren't that large, but we'd have pretty good crowds when we had a two-day special. It was a quarter-mile track. There's

This photo was too good to pass up; at the end of the Chevy row was this 1951 Chevy, which has obviously been parked in this location for a few years.I could make a pun about a "power plant," but I won't . . .

no chance that it will open again—too much work and it's much more expensive to go racing now than when we started." Besides lower dirt classes, Stateline Speedway also ran sprint car races sanctioned by the American Sprint Car Series.

Our conversation drifted back to the junkyard. I asked how they filled their property with so many cars—were they free or did they have to pay for them?

"We had to buy everything," Wanda said. "But cars back then weren't very expensive. You could buy a car for twenty dollars, and we usually had to go and get them."

I asked why they still had so many old cars. "We've never crushed any of the old stuff," she said. Then son Al chimed in. "We have a lot of people visit here from out of town," he said. "Some tourists come here occasionally from Australia and Europe. There were a bunch of them here that were part of some kind of drag racing tour, I think sponsored by *Hot Rod* magazine. But most of the people who come here are from the central states or maybe a few from California."

Al told us they didn't have a website and don't sell parts through eBay. "It's just all sitting back there," he said. "The old car-part market is tough because your perception of the condition of a forty- or fifty-year-old part and a buyer's can be completely different."

Like his father, Al was also a racer. He raced full time for a number of years, usually within a 400-mile radius of their business. "I never raced on pavement," he said. "When I raced, I didn't have another job. Racing is what I did. I was able to race for a living, even though I didn't really make any money. I just survived."

But Al said the finances of racing changed to the point where it became impossible to pay the bills. He eventually hung up his helmet and came back to help run the family business when his dad became ill. "This business was my dad's life, and he didn't want to see it go away," Al said. "When I came back into the business, I realized that I had towed in, worked on, or took parts off so many of the old cars back there."

Both Wanda and Al said that people often come in to their yard looking for a project car. "We sell complete cars all the time," he said. "You just never know when somebody might walk back there and find a car they want."

"The other day a guy came in and bought a 1975 Ranchero," Wanda said.

"We had some guys buy the ribbed roofs off our 1958 Ford four-door sedans because they fit on some of the older Chryslers," Al said. "I only had four '58 Fords like that, but I could have sold more if I had them."

I asked Al the same question I asked his mom: whether he had any old cars himself.

Strange things happen in the salvage yard . . . A Corvair and a Morris Minor were caught mating. I wonder what the offspring would look like? Is this how hybrids are conceived?

In the Pontiac section of the yard, it's easy to see how complete these cars remain. For a yard that opened more than four decades ago, most of the cars still retain grilles, trim, gauges, bumpers, and glass, making many of them restoration projects.

"I used to have a couple of '55 Chevys, but when I went racing, I needed the money, so I sold them," he said. "But we're going to do something one day with that 1957 Chevy wagon that's back there."

We mentioned that we had spoken to Chuck Comer that morning, and he recommended we visit their yard. "Oh, Chuck bought a couple of Bud's old race cars," Wanda said. Small world— some of the race cars we had inspected a few hours earlier in Joplin had been built and raced out of the Purkey's garage.

Before we said goodbye to Wanda and Al Purkey, Al gave us a tour of his father's old race shop. Out of respect for his father, he said he rarely goes into his father's old garage, and when he does, he never takes other people with him.

To me, it was almost a religious experience to see shelves containing hundreds of new and used racing parts, ready-to-race engines, stacks of wheels and tires. Then he allowed us to go into his father's trophy room. Nobody spoke as we respectfully read the inscriptions on the dozens and dozens of trophies that Bud had won during his lifetime.

I looked over at Al and realized he was becoming emotional. Cars are more than the sum of their parts—they're reminders of the friends and family we love (and have lost) and often become part of the family history.

As we walked back out into the sunlight, I realized how fortunate Brian, Michael, and I were—complete strangers a few hours ago, and now we had been granted entry into the Purkey family's most sacred space.

Car people are amazing, trusting, sincere. As we drove toward Oklahoma, our fourth state, I realized that Wanda was correct—it was nearly 5 p.m. by the time we departed, and not a minute wasted.

ROUTE 66

OKLAHOMA

For me, Oklahoma is a significant state for two reasons. First, it is the fourth state that Route 66 travels through, so four states down, four to go once we enter Texas. And second, it is the state where our direction will change from predominantly southbound to westbound.

• • • • • • • •

Since leaving Chicago five days ago, we have driven just under 1,000 miles. We've met some great people and discovered an amazing number of cars and trucks. So far the trip is going according to plan. The commute from Purkey's Auto Salvage in Coffeyville, Kansas, to the Oklahoma state line was as easy as crossing the street—it's truly that close.

We arrived in Tulsa near sundown, so we sought out our hotel and started unloading our baggage from the Woody and the Ford Explorer onto the luggage cart. We were used to people coming to us and asking about the Woody, but the man who approached us wanted to discuss something else.

His name was Perri Voge, and he ambled up to us—sensing we were real car guys—and gave us some shocking information.

"I just heard that George Barris died today," he told us.

That was a shocker. I knew Barris and had written a book about fellow customizer Dean Jeffries. Barris was always around, wearing his yellow jacket as a celebrity at car shows throughout the United States. The King of Kustomizers was always there—I never expected him to pass away.

OKLAHOMA
ROUTE 66
THE ULTIMATE ROAD TRIP

HISTORIC
OKLAHOMA
US
66
ROUTE

ROUTE
US
66

Rand McNally
Auto Road Atlas
of the
United States

MOTEL

WOODY
GUTHRIE
CENTER | TULSA, OK

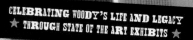
CELEBRATING WOODY'S LIFE AND LEGACY
★ THROUGH STATE OF THE ART EXHIBITS ★

OKLAHOMA
TRAVELOK.COM

Even though he and Jeffries had a lifelong rivalry and hadn't talked to each other for decades, when Jeffries passed away, Barris attended the memorial service.

I thanked Voge for the news. Then he told me he had once worked for legendary customizer George Winfield, in California.

CUSTOMIZER CONNECTION	CAR COUNT 2	FOR SALE ★ Yes ▢ No ▢ Maybe

What are the chances of meeting Perri Voge as he and his girlfriend, Tammy Sizemore, were walking into the hotel for a meeting? (Actually, when you're driving a Woody, you come to expect these sorts of things.) Voge told us he had a couple of old cars we'd probably like to see. We decided Voge's house would be our first stop in the morning.

We arrived in his driveway at about 8 a.m. and he was already waiting for us. We saw a Torino and an El Camino.

Voge is a sign painter and pinstriper, so he added vintage-looking graphics to the El Camino, making it appear as a Hurst promotional vehicle that may have once provided transportation to the likes of Linda Vaughn.

Perri Voge (left) and Tammy Sizemore met us in a hotel parking lot coincidentally on the day customizer George Barris died. They invited us over their house to see a couple of their cars.

He first showed us the Torino. "It's a 1969 Torino GT that my girlfriend owns," he said. I asked how she came to own it.

"We like old cars, and there was this guy who kept mentioning he had this old car, but none of us had ever seen it. So one day we're at a party and he told me about the car again and I said, 'Prove it.'"

The man took out his phone and showed Voge some photos. Voge said he would like to see the car, so a month or so later, the man invited him over.

"It was pretty much rust-free," he said. "He said it had belonged to a soldier who went to Vietnam and his mother kept it in her garage for thirty years. It was perfect, but when this guy got it, he left it out in the Oklahoma sun and it got baked."

The 81,000-mile car is powered by a 351 and has factory air conditioning. Sizemore has decided to sell the car. Finding a new home for a solid forty-five-year-old car shouldn't be a problem.

Remember when these Torinos were seen at every intersection and parking lot? Owner Tammy Sizemore and her boyfriend Perri "Ace" Voge found a solid example in the Tulsa area.

Voge's girlfriend, Tammy Sizemore, bought the car. Voge said he did some work on the brakes, and now it runs and drives great. The car is equipped with a 351 Cleveland, a replacement engine after the first owner blew the original engine while racing. The odometer reads 81,000 miles. "It has factory air conditioning, red body, red interior, a bench seat, and an AM/FM/tape deck," he said. "We've had it about a year." He said the car is for sale for $7,900.

Next we looked at his El Camino. "I've always liked El Caminos," he said. "I had a '59 El Camino once. I bought this one, which had been sitting for seven or eight years in an impoundment yard. It took a lot to get it running. It has a 350 and an automatic. It's my driver; I've had it for about three years."

Voge is a pinstriper and sign painter, so he lettered the vintage-looking Hurst graphics on the side. It looks like something that Linda Vaughn

would have ridden in the back of at the drag strip, waving to all her
drooling admirers.

Voge moved from Wisconsin to California in 2002 after customizer
Gene Winfield saw a chopped Mercury that Voge was building. "I've got
twelve Mercurys in California that need their roofs chopped, if you want to
come work for me," Winfield offered.

"Gene had about four employees out there in the Mojave, but nobody
knew how to fabricate and repair rust, so he and I were the only welders,"
Voge said. "I lived right in Gene's shop. I would cook one day and he
cooked the next."

Voge led us to a storage facility to show us a car his uncle owned. "This
is a 1977 Greenwood Corvette GT Sportwagon," he said. "This car has a
350 engine, gymkhana suspension, drilled-out air cleaner, racing mirrors.
This is the only blue Sportwagon Greenwood made, and the only four-speed
ever made. My uncle bought it in 1999, but his health is not good, so it will
probably be sold."

The Greenwood wagon must be rare—it's the first one I remember
seeing. We said goodbye to Voge and Sizemore and went off down the road
in search of another automotive discovery.

We posted on Facebook that we were interested in learning about any
old car leads, but most of the messages we received were not along Route
66—they came from places such as Montana or Pennsylvania. But then a
post came from a UPS deliveryman from Tulsa. He said that he passes a
yard full of Packards every day during his delivery rounds.

Works for me. Our GPS guided us to an industrial area in an older
section of Tulsa. There was no mistaking which yard our UPS driver meant—
we saw a field of Packards behind a building and several more inside.

PACKARD PACKRAT

CAR COUNT
52

FOR SALE
☐ Yes ★ No ☐ Maybe

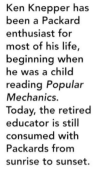

Ken Knepper has been a Packard enthusiast for most of his life, beginning when he was a child reading *Popular Mechanics*. Today, the retired educator is still consumed with Packards from sunrise to sunset.

We parked the Woody and approached the building. A woman named Oneida Knepper met us. She saw our car and assumed we were inquiring about the Packards.

"You want to speak to my husband, Ken," she said. "He's repairing the roof. I'll get him."

A few minutes later, Ken came down to meet us. Knepper told us he has been passionate about Packards since before his father purchased one off a Tulsa used car lot in 1960. "It was a 1955 Senior Packard and had five chrome wire wheels, factory air-conditioning, and two four-barrel carburetors," he said. "I think he paid two hundred seventy-five dollars for it."

Knepper still has that car in the back. "But I discovered Packards when I was a grade school student. I was in the school library reading a color

Inside Ken Knepper's shop is where he keeps his better-condition Packards and his restoration projects. He does most of the restoration work himself with the exception of paint jobs.

Knepper has a couple of custom-bodied Packards, including this ambulance, which was fabricated by Henny of Illinois. According to Knepper, the same body could function as an ambulance or a hearse.

Knepper started to buy project and parts cars in the 1960s, and still has many of those cars behind his building today. He'll only sell a part if he has others.

story in a 1955 issue of *Popular Science* about Ford, Chevy, Eldorado, and Caribbean convertibles. I knew what I wanted right then," he said.

Knepper admired the Packard's front and rear torsion bar suspension, the larger V-8 engines, and the electric push-button shifters. "I bought my first Packard on July 4, 1962," he said. "I had just graduated from high school. It was a 1956 Clipper Custom, which had a shorter wheelbase than the standard Packard. But it had all the options: power windows, power seats, power steering, rear heater, rear speaker, electric door locks. I was the second owner and still own that car."

Knepper explained to me that Packard registered the name Clipper as a separate trademark in 1956. Packard was to remain the luxury model, and the lower-end, short-wheelbase car was going to be a Clipper, not a Packard. Knepper's second Packard was a 1956 Caribbean convertible, of which he had five sitting in his garage. Knepper's father had owned Packards since 1936 and had modified several with larger engines and overdrive transmissions. His father owned a machine shop on the same premises as we were standing, which had been an auto manufacturing plant in the early 1900s for the Tulsa Four brand of automobiles and Oil Field brand trucks.

I walked around with Knepper, looking at the cars in his building. I admired a car that was actually his favorite—a three-tone 1956 400 hardtop. "A Packard V400 was a luxury hardtop, like a Cadillac Eldorado," he said. "It came with two four-barrel carburetors and limited slip differential. I bought this one in 1965."

He showed me another Packard he bought the same year. Knepper keeps his cars for a long time, and he explained that even though he owns so many Packards, it was not a business, but a hobby. He is a retired math and industrial arts teacher. Knepper and I walked out of the garage and into the backyard.

Wow. Packard two-doors, Packard four-doors, even a Packard ambulance or two.

Out to pasture: Knepper bought this Packard in 1962, when he graduated from high school. He drove it for many years before retiring it after a collision.

He explained that the ambulances, which were bodied by the Henney Motor Company of Freeport, Illinois, could be outfitted as either ambulances or hearses.

As we toured through his parts cars, he showed us the 1955 Packard that his dad purchased in 1960. Gone were the wire wheels (although Knepper said he has them indoors); gone was the pretty black-and-white, two-tone paint job. "My dad drove this until 1972," he said. Then he showed me the 1956 Clipper he bought in 1962. It had collision damage from 1980 when a lady hit her accelerator instead of the brake pedal. It's sad how these two cars have deteriorated.

I asked Knepper if he ever sold parts. "I'd only sell a part if someone really needed it and I thought that I would never need it. Yeah, I'd sell. But I try not to," he said.

His parts car collection was made up of cars that he had purchased locally, cars he found in *Hemmings Motor News*, and cars he heard about through word of mouth. He pointed out a car that he had purchased out of the state of Washington.

When we left Knepper's, we certainly knew more about Packards than we knew before. We said goodbye to Ken and Oneida and headed out. We were hungry and wanted to find a traditional Route 66 restaurant with some charm.

We found it all right.

◆ HAPPY BURGER ◆

Happy Burger is an historic restaurant built in 1957 in a classic, Route 66 style. Today the burger joint is owned by Peggy Sue Eaton (isn't that name perfect?) and is staffed by her son, JJ Mangrum, the burger chef.

While in Oklahoma, we stopped in Chandler and swung by the office of Jerry McClanahan. McClanahan wrote the guidebook, *EZ66: Route 66 Guide for Travelers*, that Brian has been using to keep us on Route 66 for our long trip. McClanahan must have driven this road a dozen times, because he points out a huge number of points of interest, turn-by-turn instructions, and suggestions on where to eat and where to stay. He even recommends sections of Route 66 to avoid because of the rough surface.

McClanahan was not there when we stopped by his office, but we admired the 1957 Chevy station wagon he had parked next to the building. If you are planning to take a Route 66 adventure, we recommend you purchase one of his route books. Go to www.mcjerry66.com.

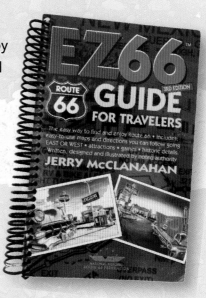

We sat at the counter and chatted with Mangrum about Happy Burger's history and his secrets in preparing the perfect burger and fries.

If you visit, go for the classic quarter-pound cheeseburger, fries, and a Pepsi (no Coke!). You won't regret it, and you'll be dining on the same meal as folks have been enjoying at Happy Burger for nearly six decades.

After lunch, we rolled on. There are sections of "Old" Route 66 that parallel the current Route 66 in Oklahoma. We drove on the older pavement when possible, but it was bumpy concrete—the Woody (and its driver) hate bumpy concrete. On the old road, we passed houses and other buildings that could tell amazing stories. I got the feeling that mine was not the first 1939 Ford Woody to traverse this route, although probably the first in a long, long time.

◆ SEABA'S MOTORCYCLE MUSEUM ◆

After lunch we explored one of the points of interest from Jerry McClanahan's Route 66 guidebook, Seaba's Motorcycle Museum, in Warwick, Oklahoma. The museum is run by an individual and operates on donations and the sale of souvenirs.

Seaba's has a nice selection of old bikes, including a brand-new and still crated Triumph Bonneville. It also sold some terrific Route 66 "Route Beer" and crème soda. It's worth a visit.

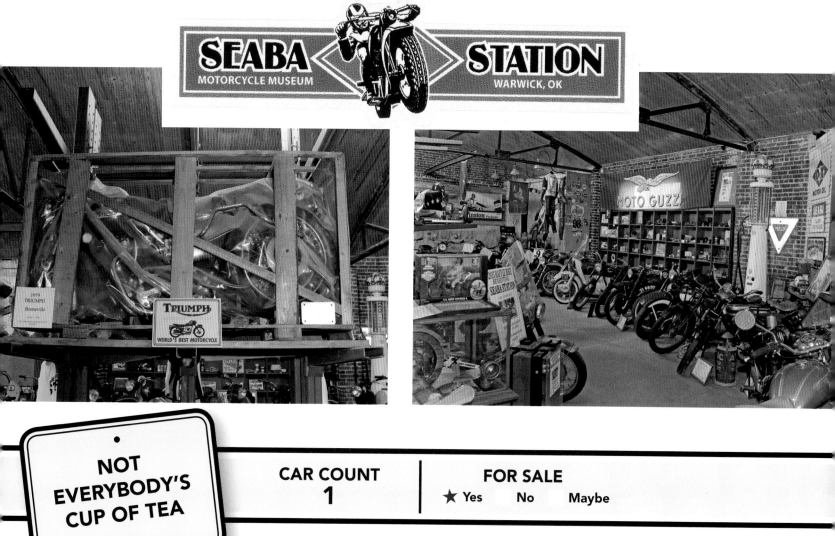

SEABA STATION
MOTORCYCLE MUSEUM
WARWICK, OK

NOT EVERYBODY'S CUP OF TEA

CAR COUNT	FOR SALE
1	★ Yes No Maybe

We passed an old Chevy Vega that was for sale on the side of the road. Not only are Vegas rare these days, this was a *Cosworth* Vega. This one was a 1977 model with an engine developed by famed English racing engine supplier, Cosworth. The company was founded by Mike Costin and Keith Duckworth to develop Formula One engines for Ford Motor Company in the 1960s.

This car seemed to be complete, including the correct Cosworth Vega alloy wheels and the serial number badge on the dashboard. It was car number 1,308 of 3,508 manufactured.

The Cosworth Vega was a performance and style upgrade for GM's economy car, but it never lived up to expectations. Government regulations limited the horsepower from a hopeful 140 to 110.

The "For Sale" sign says 1977, but actually the 3,508 Cosworth Vegas were only built in 1975 and 1976.

The asking price of $2,700 seemed reasonable for the project, but it is unclear from the sign whether the engine and gearbox that are included with the sale are the correct and original Cosworth units, or standard Vega components. It could make quite a difference in the price.

Continuing west on Route 66, we noticed another unusual sight: a Volkswagen Beetle sticking out of the second story of a building! It was certainly worth a visit.

| HOT ROD SCULPTOR | CAR COUNT 5 | FOR SALE ☐ Yes ★ No ☐ Maybe |

One of the most interesting people we met on our trip, John Hargrove has quite an imagination and the talent to build what he imagines.

We drove into the driveway, not knowing if we were entering a commercial establishment, a private home, or a tourist destination. It turned out to be all three!

From the building where the VW was sticking out walked a gentleman named John Hargrove. Hargrove looks like your average older fellow, but we discovered that he was not only a hot rodder, but a sculptor, a restorer, an upholsterer, and an athlete!

He showed us several of his cars, starting with a chopped 1932 Ford two-door sedan. "It was built in California in the early 1950s," he said. "I've had it since about 1974. I bought it in Oklahoma as a drag car at the fairgrounds out here. It ran the quarter-mile as a B-Altered. I bought only the body shell and two outside frame rails. It was completely gutted on the inside. Thank goodness they left the doorposts in place."

Hargrove had his work cut out for him. In order to make it a street car again, he had to move the firewall forward from the doorposts to the front cowl. He also had to rebuild the interior panels.

You'll never find another one! Hargrove built this car, utilizing the front-wheel-drive system from a late-model GM car and the rear suspension from a motorcycle. The body is homemade of fiberglass.

"I built a street rod out of it, but changed the outside as little as I could," Hargrove said. "It was a typical junkyard build, and it was rough. But the grille is the same grille that was in it."

Hargrove said the '32 raced with a 409-cubic-inch engine and a Powerglide transmission during its drag days. The driver's seat was relocated all the way to the back of the car, and it had blue plexiglass screwed to the window frames. He said it raced and won in the 1964 Texas Winternationals with a driver named Gale Reed. These days the deuce sedan is powered by a 305 Chevy with a Turbo 400 transmission.

Next to the hot rod sedan, Hargrove showed us his 1914 Model T Ford roadster. I asked him when he restored it, and he told me he doesn't think it's ever been restored. "It's got a hot rod engine in it, a 1926 Model engine with a high compression head with a Model A crankshaft," he said. It also has a Ruckstell two-speed differential. "See that interior?" he pointed out. "That's original. Or at the least it was upholstered a very long time ago."

He then brought us into his fabrication room and showed us a replica Miller-looking Indy car he is constructing from a Model A frame. He said it has a Model A engine with a supercharger from a late-model Pontiac, a Winters Quickchange rear, and a Chevy S10 transmission will power it. He plans to install an electric water pump.

This is the VW that got our attention. It is mounted on the second floor of John Hargrove's building and is accessible from the inside for guests who come to Hargrove's catering hall.

A contrast in designs: Hargrove's 1914 Model T roadster on the left rolled off the Ford assembly line eighteen years before his chopped, ex-drag car 1932 Ford sedan.

We followed Hargrove to another building where he had a 1929 Ford pickup hot rod project that he was just finishing. It was sitting in his upholstery shop. This guy is quite an entrepreneur.

He also has an old-fashioned diner-type meeting room that can be used by clubs. Upstairs over that meeting room, Hargrove had that VW Beetle body mounted on the side of the building and people were even allowed to climb inside the bug's front seats.

Just as we were getting ready to leave, Hargrove asked why I was limping. I told him it was a running injury, and Hargrove told me he runs too. Quite seriously, in fact. Hargrove has competed in more than three hundred marathons or longer races, and twenty-five 100-mile races, including the Badwater 100, a 100-mile race through Death Valley and up a mountain! Truly an amazing guy.

As we left, he told us to visit Pop's Soda Shop, a gas station up the road that sells more than five hundred varieties of cold soda.

As silly as this sounds, this is really a cool place where you can order a

meal, get fuel, or tour their many coolers in search for bottles of soda you haven't seen since you were a kid.

◆ SATURDAY, NOVEMBER 7, 2015 ◆

The morning of the seventh day of our trip was the coldest morning yet—36 degrees. The Woody has an amazing heater, but it also allows amazing drafts to blow through the interior.

So while our toes might be toasty, our heads could be freezing. The interior drafts became especially bad whenever we passed large vehicles; the interior wind currents were pretty outrageous.

When we hit the road on Saturday morning, we drove past the town hall in Weatherford, Oklahoma, where they feature a turbine blade from a windmill lying sideways as a tourist attraction.

It was amazing. When you see those beautiful turbines spinning in the distance, it's hard to tell just how tall they are, but when you see a blade lying on the ground and can walk next to it, the size is enormous.

I drove the Woody next to the blade and it dwarfed the car. I paced off an estimated 150 feet in length. The blade made the 17-foot Woody look like a Hot Wheels toy.

◆ BUSTED! ◆

No, not because we did anything illegal. I merely needed to make a cell phone call for a one-hour interview with Bob Long's *AutoWorld* radio program. When I spoke to him earlier in the week, he wanted some updates on how our trip was going.

The problem was that even though my cell phone indicated that it had full power, I couldn't make a phone call. And as the clock ticked down to 10 a.m., I didn't know what to do. I walked into the Oklahoma Highway Patrol station in Clinton and told the lady behind the counter, Kathy Alexander, my dilemma.

"Welcome to Western Oklahoma," Kathy said, who worked as the dispatcher. "Cell phone coverage around

I normally wouldn't seek out a highway patrol headquarters on a Saturday morning, but I had a prearranged radio interview and no cell phone coverage. So I stopped in to see where I could make a call.

Dispatcher Kathy Alexander said that I could use the phone in the headquarters. After she heard the interview, she said had inherited an interesting old Ford truck from her late father, which he used to haul his drag cars to the track.

Kathy's son Cody said he would like to rebuild his grandfather's truck mechanically, but retain the exterior patina, probably coating it with clearcoat.

here is completely hit or miss. You can come into the office and use our landline. Nobody will mind."

Lucky break—I was able to make the phone call and stay warm at the same time. I spent an hour with Bob on the radio, answering questions about the trip, how many miles we'd driven, what kind of and how many old cars we had found.

When I finished the interview, Kathy asked me about the old cars she heard me discussing on the phone. "That's so interesting," she said. "I have an old truck at my house you might be interested in."

I didn't want to disappoint her, but another rusty old truck was not what I wanted.

LICENSE-LOSING COBRA JET

CAR COUNT	FOR SALE
1	☐ Yes ★ No ☐ Maybe

"I inherited it from my father," she said. "He used to haul his drag car to the strip with this truck. It has a 428-cubic-inch Cobra Jet engine in it."

I was sold! This old truck featured a bizarre engine swap and family history to boot!

"I was born and raised in this area," she said. "My father bought this truck new in 1965. We called

When the 1965 Ford truck's original engine blew, Kathy's father had the dealer install this 428 Cobra Jet. After hearing the story of the truck and the engine, it was a no-brainer to include it in this book.

it Ethyl. It had a camper on the back, and he towed a utility trailer with all his tools and the race car. The local Ford dealership was the sponsor on my father's race cars."

She told me that her father raced a variety of cars—all Fords—including a Boss 429 and a Pinto. "He set track records with that Boss 429 all over the United States," she said. His truck didn't come with the 428 engine, but when he blew up the original engine, the dealer installed the bigger engine.

She said the truck was sitting outside at her house. It's red with a white top and has a four-speed manual transmission.

I asked her if her father ever drag raced that truck. "No, he didn't, but I did," she said. "That's how I lost my driver's license when I was sixteen years old."

I asked if she would consider restoring the truck, but because oil prices were so low, she said it's on the backburner. Kathy's husband, Larry, and son, Cody, work in the oil industry, and with prices so low, there just wasn't any extra money for old-truck restorations in the near future. "We probably won't repaint it, but clearcoat it," she said. "That way we'll preserve some of the history of the truck. We would just restore it mechanically and redo the interior."

Because she was working, Kathy gave us directions to her house, where we met Larry and Cody. Larry recently completed a restoration of her father's 1953 Ford Jubilee tractor, which celebrated the fiftieth anniversary of the Ford Motor Company, which was founded in 1903. Cody, who loves pickup trucks, is considering restoring his grandfather's old Ford one day.

We counted down the miles until we got to Texas. Texas marked our halfway milestone with four states behind us and four to go. So here we were, just seven miles from Texas, and we passed a bunch of rusty hulks on the side of the road.

We had to stop.

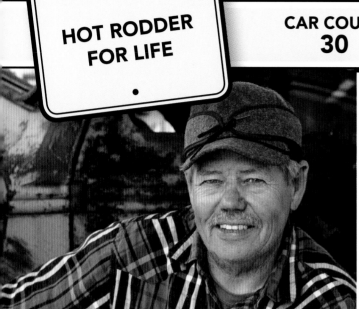

Rod Smith, who had a real tough childhood, has prospered in the oil business and now can enjoy his automotive passions full time. For a car guy, Rod Smith has achieved the American dream.

We pulled our vehicles into the driveway of a house that sat next to a row of rusty cars. A woman was just exiting her car with two small children in tow. I introduced myself and learned her name was Mrs. Smith.

"Oh, you need to speak to my husband, Rod," she said. "The cars belong to Rod and my father, who used to operate a salvage company on the property." She pointed the way to the garage where her husband, Rod Smith, was fiddling with some old cars.

Rod was an interesting guy. He was abandoned and homeless as a child and lived in cars or simply wherever he could find some shelter. He never graduated from high school. Later, he moved to Pennsylvania and New York, following opportunities in the oil business.

What's past is past, though. He must have been good at something because his home and property were impressive.

I learned the whole story. He was just a car-crazy kid who worked in gas stations until he got involved in the oil business. Then he invented

Smith has an ideal workshop, loaded with numerous restored cars, hot rods, and Corvettes. And the occasional World War II Ford-built Jeep.

Visitors to Smith's house are greeted by this display of a bikini-clad mannequin and the rusty 1938 Ford pickup that Smith and his wife used to drive on dates.

and patented a piece of equipment that didn't allow any fumes or vapor to escape from an oil rig and into the atmosphere. He said he made a small fortune.

Smith took us for a tour of his cars, starting with a rusty old 1938 Ford pickup. "I'm going to fix that up," he said. "My wife and I dated in that truck."

Then we walked past a Model A sedan and a T-bucket. Despite their rusty surfaces, the condition of the cars was amazing even though they were more than eighty years old.

We walked into his garage and he showed us a yellow '32 Ford coupe that was a dead ringer of the car in George Lucas's *American Graffiti*. "It's got a 383 stroker Chevy engine that puts out about nine hundred horsepower," he said. *Nine hundred.*

Smith started the car so we could hear the rump-rump idle—that was old-school music to our ears.

Then he showed us a 1957 Chevy two-door hardtop that appeared to be freshly restored, but it had a built-up small-block with two four-barrels. It had air conditioning and a one-piece California bumper without seams. "I've been a hot rodder my whole life, but I never had the money to own cars like this until I got older," he said.

We walked into the next building. There, Smith had a Model A pickup, roadster, and sedan; a 1940 Chevy; and a World War II Ford Jeep. In another room, Smith showed us his 1961 Corvette.

Smith built this *American Graffiti* 1932 Ford replica. He says it is the highest horsepower vehicle he owns; the stroked 383 cubic inch produces about 900 horsepower. I would like to do just one holeshot in this car.

Then we walked through the woods behind his house. There was a 1938 Ford pickup and some sort of postwar Dodge. "When I was a kid, in this part of the country there used to be Model As all over the place," he said. "You just don't see them anymore."

Smith explained that many of the Model Ts were bought up by the Ditch Witch Company, which used Model A rear ends in their machines. "But the old cars that you do find out here just sit—they don't rust out like they do back east."

Open wide and say Aaaaaaah. This Corvair and the Chevy sedan next to it are part of a field of cars that are owned by Smith's father-in-law. Smith said occasionally his wife's father sells cars from this lot.

We walked around Smith's fifteen acres as he continued to show us more. He revealed a 1955 Chevy pickup, 1951 Chevy fastback, and a 1942 Chevy coupe, a rare car that was built for only six months before World War II started.

Smith told us that magazines such as *Sports Illustrated* have used his property and cars for backgrounds for photo sessions.

A future project car in Smith's "holding" area is this 1951 Chevy Fleetline fastback, certainly one of the prettiest American automobile designs of the 1950s.

We walked next door to his father-in-law's property, where a couple of rows of rusty cars were. "My wife's father is retired, but he still works in that barn over there restoring old windmills," he said.

First in line on his father-in-law's property were an Opel, Chevy Nova, Corvair, 1955 Ford, split-window VW van, 1946 Ford, 1952 Ford, 1935 Ford, 1957 Chevy, and more. It was quite a discovery to make as we were dashing to exit the state.

"When I was a kid, people would come through town on Route 66 and break down," he said. "I could buy their 1955, '56, or '57 Chevy with a clear title for six dollars and fifty cents. They just needed money for a bus ride out of town."

When we arrived back at Smith's driveway, we discovered our socks and the bottom of our pants were coated with burrs. We couldn't shake them off, and if we tried to brush them away, our hands got pierced. Smith showed us how to flick them off with a knife. He loaned us his blade and told us, "I never walk in the house without taking my shoes and socks off first. My wife would kill me if these got into the carpets."

I know what he meant; the carpets in my Woody had burrs stuck to them until I was able to borrow a knife to knock them off. We said goodbye to Smith and drove the 7 miles to the Texas border.

ROUTE 66

TEXAS

Nicknamed "The Lone Star State," Texas became the 28th state on December 29th, 1845. It is ranked 2nd in size at 268,601 square miles.

I was sad to learn that Route 66 does not loop far enough south so that we could visit Midland, Texas. I have long been a fan of Jim Hall and the amazing Chaparral race cars he built in the western Texas oil town. Midland is not only the site of the Petroleum Museum, which houses Hall's collection of Chaparral Can-Am and Indy Cars, but also of Rattlesnake Raceway, where the team tested.

· · · · · · · ·

Brian said a visit to Midland would add several hundred miles to our trip, so I decided to shelve the idea. We had about one more week to get to the Santa Monica Pier, which was the official end of Route 66. So a visit to Midland, Texas, will have to wait for another time.

THE GREAT TEXAS CAR DISCOVERY

CAR COUNT	FOR SALE		
62	★ Yes	■ No	■ Maybe

After crossing the Oklahoma/Texas state line, Route 66 led us to a quiet little town named Shamrock. Soon after entering the town, we spotted a fenced-in lot loaded with old cars. It was late Saturday afternoon, nobody was around, and neither a phone number nor sign could be found.

Texas
STATE LINE

the BIG
TEXAN
STEAKRANCH

CAFE

TEXAS
ROUTE
US
66
MAIN STREET OF AMERICA

©ZAK'SLLC

Get Your Kicks on Route 66

Seeing this storage lot filled with old cars was a welcome sight soon after crossing the Texas border into the town of Shamrock from Oklahoma. We had no idea who owned it, but found out an hour later.

This was too good an automotive discovery to simply pass by, so after confirming that there were no guard dogs inside, we climbed the fence and walked around.

When trespassing, it's important you make it obvious that you are not sneaking around. Big difference between a *sneak* and a *wander*. Park your car right out front in full view of the public. Don't carry tools with you. Keep your hands in your pockets, or in Michael's case, keep your camera visible. You take these precautions so a passing police officer or some local yahoo won't think you're up to no good.

We counted sixty-two cars inside that fence! In no particular order, this is what we found:

1 1940 Chevy Sedan Delivery
3 1946–1948 Chevys (1 two-door, 2 coupes)
1 1956 Chevy
5 1957 Chevys
2 1958 Chevys
2 1959 Chevys (1 El Camino, 1 sedan)
1 1961 Chevy Bubbletop
3 Corvairs (2 sedans and 1 station wagon)
4 1964 Chevrolets
2 Chevelles
1 Pontiac Catalina
1 Ford Model A roadster

A car you don't see every day, a 1956 Hudson. This example seemed to be solid and straight and probably worthy of refurbishment to the right person.

Another rare one was this 1940 Chevy Sedan Delivery. Half car and half delivery van, these vehicles are loved by restorers and hot rodders alike. This one would take a craftsman with lots of talent and imagination to restore.

1 1958 Ford
19 Edsels (convertibles, station wagons, two- and four-door sedans)
1 Ford Falcon
1 1964 Ford
1 1966 Ford
2 Plymouths (1 Savoy, 1 Plaza)
1 1960 Chrysler
1 Hudson
4 Studebakers (3 sedans and a flatbed truck)
2 Kaisers
2 MGBs
1 small-block Chevy-powered dune buggy
And many 1950s Ford and GM trucks

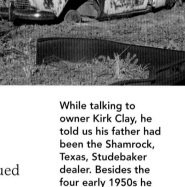

While talking to owner Kirk Clay, he told us his father had been the Shamrock, Texas, Studebaker dealer. Besides the four early 1950s he had in his lot, he also has a Golden Hawk at home.

With nobody near to answer questions about the cars, we continued driving through the town of Shamrock. We stopped at a wonderfully restored art-deco-designed gas station and café in the middle of town to take some photos.

As we were shooting, a gentleman drove past in a beautifully restored 1968 Plymouth Barracuda convertible. A few minutes later, he came by again and stopped to look at the Woody and talk with us. His name was Buc Weatherby, a former radio executive and current mayor of Shamrock. "Hi, I'm the mayor of Shamrock," he said. "Welcome to our town."

The only cars more popular than Studebakers in Clay's lot were Edsels. His father was also the local Edsel dealer, and he had collected nineteen. One of the cars in his lot was the Edsel he drove to high school.

We admired Weatherby's car—it shined in the sun, a perfect shade of metallic blue with chrome Cragar S/S wheels.

He told us about the restored gas station, which he said is one of the top six Route 66 historic sites. "This building houses the Chamber of Commerce, a gift shop, and an information center," he said.

Weatherby grew up in Shamrock, but left to manage radio stations around the country, ultimately settling in Jacksonville, Florida. He moved back to his hometown nine years ago when his mother fell ill. "You would not believe all the car people this town attracts," he said. "Our big weekend is St. Patrick's Day, when we host a car show right here." Weatherby was certainly a great goodwill ambassador for the town of Shamrock. When I asked about the cars

Clay and his father started to collect old Edsels decades ago. His father's Edsel/Mercury dealership was just a block off Route 66, around the corner from Clay's "hobby" shop today.

we had just discovered up the street, he said he would be glad to connect us with the gentleman who owned them.

Across the street from the restored gas station was another group of cars parked at a body shop, including a Studebaker, a 1959 Ford, a couple of Cushman Scooters, an old Plymouth, and an MGB. Mayor Weatherby told us the same gentleman owned those cars as well.

Convenient, I thought.

He gave us the phone number of Kirk Clay, the owner of all the cars. I called Clay a few weeks later and we had a wonderful conversation. "I wish I had known you were coming through," he said. "I would have loved to have met you."

I asked Clay how he came to own so many old cars. "My father and I used to buy old cars when we found them," he said. "He was the local Edsel dealer in Shamrock, so that's why there are so many in my lot, including the 1958 I drove to high school. He was also a Studebaker dealer in the 1940s, which is why I have a few of those."

Clay told me that beside the cars on the east end of town and in the body shop (now closed), he also has cars at home and in buildings around town. "I have a 1941 LaSalle and a 1939 Ford two-door sedan in a building, and at home I have my two favorite cars—a 1958 Chevy Impala and a 1938 Pontiac four-door sedan with suicide doors."

Certainly a rare one in anybody's book is this Edsel Pacer convertible. Owner Clay said that he often sells cars and parts to folks who need them.

One of the most iconic sites along Route 66 is this restored former Conoco gas station. Known as the Tower Building, it was constructed in the 1930s and today is on the Texas Historical Registry. It houses Shamrock's Chamber of Commerce.

Clay said he sells parts or whole cars, and that people find him through word of mouth. "I've sold most of my nice Edsels, including a few convertibles," Clay said. "I've spent most of my life on Route 66, from 1957 until last year. Since I retired, I've had two open-heart surgeries, and that has slowed me down. But I'm feeling better and want to get back on working on my old cars."

Texas is a huge state, but the northern section through which Route 66 passes through is only about 150 miles wide. So after Shamrock, we continued westbound toward Amarillo, the only major Texas city we would be passing through.

Two steakhouses stood within easy walking distance from our hotel. Now, how can you go to Texas and not eat at a steakhouse? One of the choices was Outback, the other was Hoffbrau Steaks. Hoffbrau was the easy choice, and we sat at the bar. Where else?

Our favorite bartender of the trip, Schuyler Cochran, who tends bar at the Hoffbrau Steaks in Amarillo, Texas. The stuffed armadillo is her pet. (An Amarillo armadillo?)

Our bartender was an energetic young lady named Schuyler Cochran. She was a Texas native and the ideal barkeep. She told us about Amarillo, but couldn't tell us about any old cars in the area.

Regardless, she entertained us, made recommendations on beer, and suggested we order the filet. So we ordered the filet, and it was perfect.

It was an ideal meal for the one night we'd be staying in Texas.

◆ SUNDAY, NOVEMBER 8, 2015 ◆

The next morning was Sunday, the beginning of our second week on the road. So far we had driven 1,439 miles without any mechanical issues except for a sticky ignition switch that occasionally needed a smack from Brian's pocketknife. Our fuel mileage was about 21–22 miles per gallon. Pretty good, I would say, for a seventy-six-year-old car with the aerodynamics of a shoebox.

Because it was Sunday, our expectations were not high about finding anything that morning. One car attraction we did want to visit, however, was Cadillac Ranch, the internationally renowned automotive-themed sculpture in which a series of vintage Cadillacs have their noses buried in the ground and their tails pointed toward the sky.

A do-not-miss attraction while in Amarillo, Texas, is Cadillac Ranch, located along the I-40 service road just south of the interstate. The internationally known installation has ten vintage Caddys buried up to their windshields, tails pointed to the sky.

Early Sunday morning we met two young ladies, college students from Houston, who wanted to leave their marks on history. Leigh Milbauer (left) and Alyssa Amador brought along spray cans from Walmart.

Michael and I got up early (pre-dawn—yikes!) and drove a few miles from our hotel to the Cadillac Ranch site. Brian decided to sleep in that morning.

Other people started arriving before the sun rose above the horizon. This place has a mystical, almost spiritual aura. It has become an American version of Stonehenge, where people come to see the Cadillacs at sunrise, sunset, and in the middle of the night. Many carry cans of spray paint and leave their own marks on the half-buried cars.

While we were shooting photos, two young ladies, Leigh Milbauer and Alyssa Amador, college students from Houston, arrived with spray cans. They were making a circumnavigational road trip around Texas in their red Chevy Sonic.

"When you look up things to do in Amarillo, this is like the top three," Amador said. "We bought paint at Walmart on the way here. You normally can't spray-paint anything legally, so we really wanted to do this."

◆ WESTBOUND AND DOWN ◆

We were drawn into a wind farm that had no gates or fences. We were told that the turbines make huge wind noise, but standing underneath one, it made no more noise than a truck going down the freeway. I call it mechanical poetry.

Besides the fact it was Sunday—which barn-finders should often consider as a day of rest as well—Texas was so barren along Route 66 that we just didn't find many old cars from Amarillo to the New Mexico border. There are miles and miles of nothing—no homes, no businesses, no roads. There was just prairie land and the occasional windmill farm. It took two hands on the steering wheel to keep my wooden box of a car between the lines.

We followed Route 66 when we could, but sometimes it just came to an end because of a washed-out bridge or simply lack of pavement.

The blowing wind must be constant and unending because the few trees we saw only had visible growth only on the north side because of the strong winds from the south. And as uncomfortable as Brian and I were inside the windy Woody, I can't imagine how hearty the original settlers were who pioneered their way through this land as they tried to farm and work through the various oil booms and busts.

Anyway, I'm sure we could have discovered more old cars west of Amarillo if we had more time and the opportunity to venture from Route 66. But time was of the essence and we had to keep going.

Many of the small towns we did pass through had rusty trucks scattered about. If we had stopped to photograph all of them, we'd still be on the road! Thus far it has been easier to discover old cars on the earlier part of our adventure. The huge expanses of western Texas made discoveries less frequent. Then again, we've noticed the condition of the cars in the West were much better than the cars we found to the east and north. So the automotive reward may be worth the search.

On to New Mexico!

We had to stop right on the pavement! Even though we had driven about 1,500 miles as the result of chasing down leads on old car finds, we had officially completed 50 percent of Route 66, halfway from Chicago to LA.

The Three Stooges: Brian (left), me (center), and Michael pose for a group photo, having completed half our journey, 1,139 miles, with 1,139 miles to go!

ROUTE 66

NEW MEXICO

W e were right on target, according to the crude schedule I devised several weeks before the trip. My hope was to arrive in New Mexico after one week on the road, with one more week and three states to go. This was our eighth day on the road with one week to go—right on schedule.

· · · · · · · ·

I love it when a plan comes together.

We're optimistic about our chances of automotive discoveries in New Mexico. Several people along the route had told us that the town of Tucumcari had a few old cars on Route 66 that we shouldn't miss. As we pulled into town late Sunday afternoon, we passed a fenced-in lot on the left side that was filled with a variety of vintage tin. This time, though, two guard dogs were inside the fence. Clearly no Shamrock, and no mayor or (mayoral candidates) in sight.

I noticed a sign with a phone number and figured *what the heck*. I called the number and spoke with Danny Ellis, who said he'd be glad to meet us at 9 a.m. the next morning.

Terrific. With our first discovery arranged, we searched for lodging and a meal for the evening.

DANNY'S HOBBY CARS

CAR COUNT	FOR SALE
21	☐ Yes ☐ No ★ Maybe

We arrived at Ellis's building at 9 a.m. on the ninth day of the Route 66 Barn Find Road Trip and he was already waiting for us. We walked into the building to introduce ourselves and he started to tell us about his life. "I'm not in business," he said. "I'm retired and this is my hobby. I rent out land for a bunch of wind turbines on some property I own, so I get a check every month."

He pointed toward a mountain several miles behind his shop that he leases for eight wind turbines and 2,200 solar panels. "The checks won't make us rich, by any means, but it allows us to live a comfortable life," he said.

We arrived late on Sunday afternoon to find a yard we had heard about from several people. The gate was locked and two dogs were very much on the job. We made arrangements to meet owner Danny Ellis the next morning.

Danny Ellis worked hard all his life, and he now enjoys working and collecting old cars full time in his retirement.

Our conversation quickly turned to cars. "There are still plenty of old cars out there, but they are not on Route 66," Ellis said. "I had to drag these in from around the area. If you travel fifty miles south, or fifty miles north of here, you can still find old cars. Most of the cars I have come from about ninety miles south of here."

Danny told us of one unique way to acquire old vehicles—be the beneficiary in someone's will. "I had a friend who passed at ninety-four years old, and I was in his will. He had one hundred twenty-five cars, some tractors, and some trucks. The will said that I could buy any and all the cars I wanted for the price in a ledger."

I asked Ellis if he would consider selling any cars in his yard. "Nothing is for sale," he said. "Well, let me correct that—the majority are not for sale. I have a Chevy Suburban that I would sell, and there is a DeSoto I'd sell."

Ellis was working on two 1956 Chevys, a two-door and this four-door, which he had recently acquired. After he gets the heater system working correctly, he plans to use the car as a daily driver.

Probably the most intriguing car in Ellis's lot was this supercharged Graham Paige. The design is amazing, and the supercharger, more common on Mercedes and Duesenberg models, was unheard of for blue-collar American cars.

Ellis told us stories of his youth and what it was like growing up along Route 66 in the 1950s. "I saw people whose cars broke down on the highway," Ellis said. "The husband would be working on the old Chevy, the oil pan would be down. The wife would be cooking a meal, and there would be a tarp against the fence to cut the wind. They had to save the engine oil in mason jars so they could use it again. They had to fix themselves a home in their car until it was fixed."

Amazing. It's hard to even fathom in this day and age.

Ellis's dad was totally blind, but he ran an auto repair garage about 30 miles west of Tucumcari. "He did everything by feel. He would install points, fix generators, starters, carburetors, whatever needed to be done. My mom would help him out if he needed it."

Ellis grew up in a wooden building without a bathroom or running water. "But when you grow up like that, you don't know any difference," he said. "We grew up poor, but we didn't know we were poor because everyone else was poor."

I fell in love with Nashes on this trip. Here is a solid 1953 Ambassador Custom model with Italian styling by Farina that would be an easy restoration. Next to it is a nice "Job-Rated" Dodge pickup.

Above: Ellis certainly had enough Studebakers. Here is a lineup of Larks, including two- and four-doors, a wagon, and a pickup truck.

Below: A collection of old cars wouldn't be complete without a Model A Ford. Ellis had this one, which was amazingly complete and appeared to be a runner.

Above: My favorite car in Ellis's yard was this 1935 Studebaker President sedan. The car was more stylish than most American cars of the day. It would be a tough restoration, too.

Below: Ellis had a couple of Crosleys, including this pickup. The engines in these vehicles were small, light, and stout. Many were utilized in Midget race cars and speedboats.

Ultimately, Ellis built a business in dirt—buying, selling, and moving it. He bought a front-end loader and remained in that business until he retired a few years ago. He has always been a car enthusiast, though, especially for Studebakers. He goes to national Studebaker shows and has made a number of trips to the Studebaker Museum in South Bend, Indiana.

We started to walk around his shop. "I'm working on this '56 Chevy two-door hardtop right now," he said. "I bought it for twenty dollars in 1972. It didn't have an engine or transmission or a hood. And I found that '56 Chevy four-door hardtop about six months ago near the city dump," he said, pointing to the car. "I just cleaned it up; it's got a 265 Powerglide."

We walked outside and Danny told me about some of his cars. "That is a supercharged Graham Paige," he said. "It has a gear-driven fan belt that drives the blower."

MAGIC STRIPPER

Before we departed, Ellis wanted to make sure we saw his magic stripper, which is something I would like to tell everybody too—*come check out the stripper!* Ellis was a gentleman, however, and referred only to his environmentally safe paint and rust stripping system. He showed us a fifty-five gallon drum filled with some kind of liquid. Sitting in the barrel was an old pickup truck tailgate. Only about 5 inches of the tailgate was exposed—the rest was submerged in the liquid.

When he pulled the tailgate out of the liquid, it was perfectly stripped of all paint and rust, right down to the raw metal. "It's just water and molasses from our local feed supply," Ellis said. "Farmers use it to mix with grain for their cattle. It's totally safe for the environment. It is oxygen-seeking, so it strips everything

Ellis showed us his molasses-based paint and rust stripping method. Take a look at this tailgate that he has soaked for a couple of weeks; look at the metal on the lower part: fresh, clean metal.

down the metal. If it rains and overflows, it doesn't do any harm. A fifty-pound bag of powdered molasses costs about twenty dollars. The dogs come over here and drink it because it's sweet."

Thanks to Danny Ellis for that tip.

A number of Studebakers were in his yard, including sixteen Larks, a Henry J, a Nash Ambassador, three Metropolitans, a Crosley pickup truck, and a dozen other cars. My favorite was the 1934 Studebaker President. The car was so much more stylish than the Fords, Chevys, or Dodges of that era, and it seemed almost European in appearance. It had a straight-eight engine and a free-wheeling transmission.

I have to admit that the only time I had heard of the town of Tucumcari prior to driving through it was from the song "Willin,'" originally performed by Little Feat in 1971, but later covered by Linda Ronstadt (1974), Jon Randall (1999), and Steve Earle (2002).

It was a pretty cool town. We stayed in a local hotel and enjoyed a wonderful steak dinner and a couple of beers.

The next morning we aimed the Woody westward toward the next sizable town—Santa Rosa. We passed many old cars on Historic Route 66 between Tucumcari and Santa Rosa—this was the route as it existed prior to 1937.

Believe it or not, this is actually a piece of Historic Route 66, unpaved, dusty, and deserted.

Cars sat beside houses, behind businesses, and in fields. But either there was nobody around to talk with, or they were locked up behind a fence with "NO TRESPASSING, PRIVATE PROPERTY" signs on the gate. I'll often take chances to look at an old car if it's out in the open, but not if it means getting shot, so we probably passed one hundred old cars or more before arriving in Santa Rosa.

We were advised to visit the antique car museum in the middle of Santa Rosa right on Route 66. But I couldn't see the value of visiting a museum—our trip was a barn-find adventure, and seeing a bunch of shiny cars lined up in a building is not why you bought a copy of this book. So we decided to pass it by.

But nearly across the street from the museum was an auto center named Bozo's. At first glance, Bozo's looked like your average brake and tire specialist, but a number of old cars were in the parking lot.

I decided it was worth a visit to see who this Bozo fellow was.

BOZO'S JUNKYARD	CAR COUNT 100+	FOR SALE ★ Yes No Maybe

Bozo's is a brake and tire specialist business, but its secondary business is building hot rods. Here was a '57 Chevy and there a '58 Ford Ranchero. And a Falcon. And a Comet.

James "Bozo" Cordova, who was out of town, owns the business. So we spoke with Juan Jaramillo, second-in-command and Bozo's brother-in-law. We were standing next to the '58 Ranchero, which, according to Jaramillo,

We noticed Bozo's auto center because a few cars were parked in the front, such as this 1956 Chevy four-door "convertible." I would normally discount a car like this, but after seeing the shop's other projects, I truly believe this will become an amazing conversion.

is a car Bozo recently purchased. "He bought this about two or three months ago," Jaramillo said. "We're not going to restore it, just put it together and running so we can sell it. We'll ask about six thousand dollars for it."

Bozo's reputation for building cars brings customers from far and wide. A 1956 Ford pickup belonged to a customer in Kingman, Arizona. The shop installed a 302 Ford drivetrain in it, but will leave the cosmetics the way they are.

Patina is the new lacquer! Or as Michael says, rust is the new chrome.

Even though most of the cars at Bozo's lot are Chevys, this 1955 Ford wagon got my attention. It was solid and complete, a straight-forward restoration or rod project.

One of the 1957 Chevys being worked on in the garage was brought in by a customer from Illinois. "We're doing a lot of work to it," Jaramillo said. "He would like to sell it."

I followed Jaramillo through the back door and out to their private junkyard at the rear of the property. As we were walking, he told me that Bozo has owned this business for forty-five years.

Before walking into the yard, Jaramillo wanted to show me a 1955 Chevy Nomad they had just completed. It was sitting in their body shop. It was one of the best Nomad hot rods I have ever seen. "This car was rougher than most of the cars in the junkyard," he said.

Now, however, it had one of the best red paint jobs I've ever seen, perfect bodywork, new chrome, and an LS3 drivetrain with a six-speed transmission! Quite a transformation.

Above: Tri-Fives are us! Bozo's had lots of 1955 through '57 Chevys in their backyard. Because they have been pretty much stripped over the years, they are primarily parts cars.

Below: Bozo's has three 1956 Buick Century two-door hardtops under a shed. All three were solid, complete, and ready for refurbishment.

Above: Don't you know that some rat rodder would give his eye teeth for this International flatbed truck? Even though it was coated in surface rust, it has solid metal, although somewhat banged up.

Below: A surface-rusted Shoebox Ford Tudor. Again, don't get scared away by the rust; under the surface are solid body panels and floors.

Jaramillo said we could walk around the yard and take photos all we wanted. Before walking into the brush to inspect the junkyard, I asked Jaramillo if there were any snakes back there. "Yes, lots of them, but I already fed them today," he said with a laugh.

More than one hundred cars were in the yard, including at least twenty 1955–1957 Chevys. Three 1956 Buick Century two-door hardtops sitting under a shed got my attention. They looked so good that I wouldn't be surprised if they had fresh batteries installed, they could become daily drivers.

It is amazing how much more solid the cars have gotten since we left Illinois; every state south and west has yielded more solid bodies, floors, and even paint. If you are an old car enthusiast who lives in the Chicago area, drive 1,000 miles southwest on Route 66 before buying an old car—the condition of your project will save you a huge amount of restoration expenses.

The recently completed 1955 Chevy Nomad. We were told that the car started out as a hulk worse than anything in the yard we had looked at. Now it is powered by an LS3 and a six-speed gearbox.

After forty-five minutes out in the yard (snake-free, thankfully), I went back into the shop and asked Jaramillo if anything was for sale. "Everything is for sale, parts or whole cars," he said. After looking at the quality of the work on Bozo's own '55 Nomad, it's easy to see why customers come from as far as California to have work performed on their old cars.

As we were leaving, Jaramillo told us to make sure we stopped in the antique car museum across the street. "Bozo owns that too," he said.

"No thanks," I told him. "We've already seen all the cool stuff."

Before leaving Santa Rosa, we came upon a little yard with some old cars. A couple of rusty cars were set up like sculptures, so we stopped in.

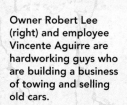

Owner Robert Lee (right) and employee Vincente Aguirre are hardworking guys who are building a business of towing and selling old cars.

WE'LL SELL 'EM, EL CHEAPO

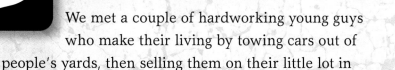

CAR COUNT	FOR SALE		
6	★ Yes	No	Maybe

We met a couple of hardworking young guys who make their living by towing cars out of people's yards, then selling them on their little lot in downtown Tucumcari. They were nice guys who were just trying to scratch out a living. I got the impression that they would give us the shirts off their backs!

The name of the business is Chavez Roadrunner, and they do auto repairs as well as haul cars. Robert Lee is the owner, and he works with Vincente Aguirre. "We go and clean people's property, and if they don't pay us, we keep and sell the old cars," Lee said. He showed us some of his

This '39 Chevy low rider was more yard sculpture than project car, but it got us off the road and into the Chavez Roadrunner yard. Check out the chrome wire wheels without tires.

One of the four Kaiser package deal cars—the cost is $3,000 for the lot. Not easy to restore or get parts for, however.

finds: a Hudson Hornet, a '39 Chevy, a rare Austin of England, a couple of Kaisers, and a bunch of 1950s Ford pickups. "Actually we have four Kaisers," Lee said. "We'd sell all four for three thousand dollars."

I asked Lee if he was a hot rodder. "I'm a low rider," he said. "At home I have a 1959 Oldsmobile Bubbletop low rider."

His sidekick, Aguirre, said he has a 1962 Ford Unibody pickup and a 1952 GMC.

"People come by here and buy parts and cars," Lee said. "We'll do whatever it takes to make a dollar."

We hit the big town of Santa Fe one night and cruised around as the sun was rising the next morning. It's a neat town where I would have liked to spend more time.

◆ TUESDAY, NOVEMBER 10, 2015 ◆

The next morning we spotted a fenced-in yard with many old cars in the town of Bernalillo, New Mexico. But it resembled an armed fortress, and I was not about to open the gate and walk in for fear of being mauled, shot, spiked, skewered . . . it looked like a dangerous place. A young man saw me peering over the fence, though, and said it was his uncle's house.

"But he doesn't sell anything and he never goes outside," he said.

Hmmm . . . strange.

Next, we saw a policewoman outside the property on Route 66 in her police cruiser checking the speed of cars on her radar as they drove by.

"Excuse me," I said. "I'm driving down Route 66 in that Woody over there looking for old cars. Do you know of any around?"

She said there was a towing company a few blocks away that has some old cars behind a fence. I thanked her and drove in that direction.

TOWING COMPANY COLLECTOR	CAR COUNT 12	FOR SALE ☐ Yes ☐ No ★ Maybe

We met Howard Sandoval, operator of the towing company. He showed us his project in the shop—a 1946 Chevy Fleetliner. "I'm installing a Chevy small-block 400 engine, disc brakes in the front and rear, an automatic transmission with a Camaro rear end," he said. "I painted it right here."

It looked black to me inside the building, but he said it was actually a very dark burgundy. "It's a one-family ownership vehicle. My older brother bought it new in 1946, got drafted in 1950, and went MIA in Korea in 1951. We never saw him again. It had been in my mother's garage until about fifteen years ago, when she gave it to me."

This car was so solid—no rust in the body or floors. Sandoval was proud of his car and should be.

Next, we walked outside his shop to find a first-edition Ford Bronco. "It's a 1973 and it's a driver," he said. "It had a 302, but I dropped a 351 Windsor in it. I've had it since about 1989. This is not for sale. These cars are my own projects."

Howard Sandoval was rightfully proud of this 1946 Chevy Fleetliner; his older brother bought it new, but never returned from the Korean War, so the car sat in his mom's garage until she gave it to her younger son, Howard.

Howard Sandoval has spent his career towing wrecks around his region of New Mexico. He is probably in the best position to find rust-free cars as he travels around.

Sandoval's "driver" 351-powered Generation 1 Bronco. With the value of these having multiplied over the past few years, collectors would love to get their hands on his rust-free New Mexico example.

Also in his tow yard was a 1951 Ford with a 289, a 1940 and a 1941 Chevy, a 1963 Buick Riviera, and a two-wheel drive Jeep station wagon. Sandoval said he is restoring a 1928 Chevy in his home garage.

After leaving Sandoval's business, we drove back to the fenced-in yard we had seen earlier, hoping to see a person walking around. No luck—nobody was inside the fence we could talk to.

But looking just a few lots west, behind a small banquet facility, we saw a bunch of cars behind another fence. Thankfully, the banquet center sign had a phone number on it, so I called it, hoping the same person who owned the cars owned it too.

With plans to mount this Jeep station wagon body on a later model S10 chassis, Sandoval said this project is next on his to-do list after the Fleetline is completed.

Bingo! It was!

I spoke to Steve Amiot, who confirmed that he owned all those old cars and he could meet us there at 3 p.m.

So with a few hours to kill, Michael said he spotted a repair shop with a few old cars behind it just down the road in a town named Bernalillo.

He called us on our cell phone from his Explorer. "Hey, did you see that old Thunderbird back there?" he asked.

"No sir," we said. He caught us off guard—who were the car hunters and who was the photographer?

So we turned around, and sure enough a few old cars were behind Alameda Tire Shop and Service. It wasn't a T-Bird, but I can understand how Michael could confuse the 1958 Ford Ranchero with a T-Bird, because both Fords had quad-headlights and square bodies.

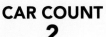

NO LOW RIDERS

CAR COUNT	FOR SALE
2	★ Yes No Maybe

Sebastian Gurule runs a tire and brake business in Bernalillo, New Mexico, but he also trades in old cars and trucks. He said that gearheads who live in New Mexico care more for originals these days than for low riders.

Another car Gurule was selling was this '51 Chrysler Windsor. It was not a Hemi car, but rather had a straight-six-cylinder flathead. But it was a two-door and could be a candidate for a cool street rod.

OK, Michael gets a pass for confusing this '58 Ranchero for a '58 T-Bird. After all, we were going 50 miles per hour and it was partially hidden behind a fence. It is a good starting point for a restoration, although the quarter panels need work.

We met Sebastian Gurule, owner of the repair shop. We told Gurule we were writing a book about finding old cars. He was all over it.

"I'm getting two V-12 Lincoln Zephyrs tomorrow, a 1947 and a 1948," he said. "They are coming from the Flagstaff area. I'll have those for sale tomorrow."

I told him we were just passing through and asked about the Ranchero. "I've had it about one year. It belonged to a neighbor who has skin cancer, so he brought it over here for me to get it running, then sold it to me," Gurule said. "It runs and drives but needs a little love, and probably some tires. I'm probably going to sell it, although I'm not in a big rush. It's an automatic 312. It has a good body, but the quarter panels have a few issues."

He told me about the car sitting beside the Ranchero: "It's a 1951 Chrysler Windsor Deluxe. It has a flathead six-cylinder Spitfire motor that runs and drives well. It's going to need brake work, maybe a master cylinder."

He said he's been working on cars his whole life: "My dad was a mechanic. I've been in this shop selling cars and tires for about three years. There are a lot of old cars here in New Mexico. Some people think they are worth a little more than they actually are, but there are a few around. People think *New Mexico* and imagine we're all low riders, but that's kind of phasing out. People today are wanting original. That's how I like them."

Gurule said his friend fixes up 1947 to 1954 Chevy pickups and makes good money selling them. "He air-bags them, puts new front ends on them, and sells them," he said. "They are

We met our Hagerty traveling companions, Claire Walters, Ben Woodward, and Jordon Lewis at the famous Owl Café, an Albuquerque landmark and local hot rod hangout. Michael and I ordered the daily special, Frito pie.

real pretty trucks. At first you don't think so, but once it's dropped and it's all patina-ed and runs like a new car, they are pretty cool."

Around noon we were scheduled to meet up with our colleagues from Hagerty Insurance, who were scheduled to fly into Albuquerque to spend a few days with us. Hagerty's video team planned to follow us around with cameras, documenting our barn-finding discoveries for a new YouTube series for their website and email newsletter. We met Claire Walters, part of Hagerty's public relations department and producer of this series, and Jordon Lewis and Ben Woodworth, Hagerty's videographers.

Rather than meet them at the airport, we decided to meet at the Owl Café, a place I had never heard of, but one that Claire had visited on a previous Route 66 trip and spoke of highly.

The Owl Café is actually shaped like an owl. It's very cool and is actually automotive-themed. I spoke to the owner, who is a hot rodder. He said that the café hosts weekly cruise-ins all summer.

We enjoyed a terrific lunch, then headed back toward Bernalillo so we could meet with Steve Amiot for our 3 p.m. appointment. Amiot had a fine selection of cars behind his fence—domestic, foreign, cars, trucks, even a celebrity car.

The Woody sits outside the Owl Café.

ELLA'S LINCOLN AND SUPPORTING CAST

CAR COUNT	FOR SALE		
23	★ Yes	No	Maybe

Before even opening the gates, Steve said we could expect a spectacular sunset and lighting on the mountains behind us.

"See those mountains over there?" he asked. "Those are called the Sandias, which in Spanish means 'watermelon.' In the evening, they turn

Steve Amiot is a car guy through-and-through. On a hobby basis, he restores, buys, and sells only cars that interest him.

One of two 1958 Chevy station wagons Steve Amiot has in his collection. The other is a restored A/C-equipped car. The good news is that just about everything he has is for sale at reasonable prices.

pink, like watermelon." Michael, Jordon, and Ben were excited to hear that.

I asked why he had so many cars. "I'm a car guy," he said. "I'm supposed to be retired from the restaurant business, but I've been doing this car stuff full-time for thirty-five years. These cars are the result. My wife says to get rid of them and let's go on a vacation, but I can't agree with her, you know?"

I sure do. We started at one end of his yard and progressed to the other, talking as we went.

We walked past an old Ford truck. I asked why the fender had been widened. "It's a '51, and it's been converted to a dually," he said. "It was a farm truck used in the southeast corner of the state. The flathead engine runs well and only needs a water pump. I call it yard art; it belongs to a friend who never intends to sell it, so it just sits in my yard."

Anyone would like this '63 Falcon Futura Sprint. The two-door hardtop is a factory V-8, four-speed car, and it had an amazingly solid body.

He walked us toward his shop, where he polishes and removes dents from stainless-steel automobile trim as a side business. He also rents one garage bay to a friend who paints cars.

He showed us his 1958 Chevy four-door station wagon, one of two he has. "This one is a Yeoman, one of the rarest Chevys there is," he said. "These are usually powered by six-cylinders, but this one has a 283 and some rare options: power brakes, super rare; power steering, super rare; factory air conditioning, super, super rare on the cheapest wagon Chevy made in 1958. This one is definitely for sale, probably in the twenty thousands."

Amiot also showed us a replica he is building of the first 1968 COPO big-block Camaro. "Don Yenko built all his 1968 Camaros from Super Sport models, but he ordered one standard model from Chevrolet with a Corvette engine installed from the factory," he said. "So this is a copy of that car."

Amiot told us about a friend in a nearby valley along the river who has two hundred cars in his yard, mostly from the thirties, forties, fifties, and a few from the sixties.

A car that got my attention was the 1954 Ford Ranch Wagon. I own a 1953 Ranch Wagon, which I bought in 1972 for $85, not because I loved it, but because it was the only car I could afford that would take me to high school! Amiot wants a reasonable $400 for his.

"He had this old Lincoln sitting in the corner, so I approached him one day and said, 'That's a pretty straight '61 Lincoln.' He said, 'Yeah, would you believe that it used to belong to jazz singer Ella Fitzgerald?'

"I said, 'No, actually I don't believe it, but it's a good story.'"

Amiot said about seventy of his friend's cars were towed away when he failed to comply with the county's old car ordinance.

"I had already bought two solid Buick Rivieras from him, a 1963 and a 1964," Amiot said. "Well, after so many of his cars were repossessed, he called and said he would like to have those Rivieras back.

"He said, 'Come on down here and see what else you want, and I'll trade for those Rivieras.'"

So Amiot went to his friend's house in the valley and clamped his eyes on a 1948 Chrysler coupe. Then he saw that Lincoln again.

"I asked if he had any proof that this was Ella's car," he said. "He said, 'Yeah, I think so.' So a week later, he showed me the original registration from the 1960s."

Amiot showed me the registration, which matched the original California black license plate. "So I thought that was cool, and I traded," he said.

He told me to look at the back seat.

"She would always sit in the right side in the back seat," he said. "Her driver would sit in the front. She never drove the car; she would only tour and sing. She had a mansion in Beverly Hills. When she would go to the Copa Cabana or *The Tonight Show*, she would always sit on curbside so she could make the grand entrance. So the back seat has an indentation where she always sat." The car only has 76,000 miles on it.

"She lived in Europe a lot, so this car was not used too much," he said. "She would perform with Dizzy Gillespie and Louis

If I only lived closer . . . Amiot wants $1,500 for this front-wheel-drive Saab Sonnet sports car. It is powered by a V-4 Ford industrial engine. I used to race my Datsun 510 against one of these and know they are great handling cars.

Of course the prize of Amiot's yard was this 1961 Lincoln Continental, bought new by jazz singer Ella Fitzgerald. The car is straight and solid and would be the ideal collector car for a jazz enthusiast.

Armstrong. Tony Bennett recently said that Ella Fitzgerald was the greatest singer he ever heard."

I asked him why he kept the windows open. He said because he didn't want condensation to develop (and because the electric windows are broken).

"We don't have much rain around here anyway," he said.

Amiot said he would sell Ella's Lincoln for $5,000. I think that is a *steal*.

Next, we moved on to the rest of his yard. A 1964 Ford Galaxie convertible was next to a Falcon Futura Sprint with a V-8 and four-speed.

"It's another one of those cars I'll probably never get to," Amiot said of the Falcon.

In another spot was a Studebaker Lark station wagon and a 1958 Pontiac. It was a barn-finder's dream. "That Pontiac is an original Santa Cruz car," he said. "I'd let that go for a grand. And the Lark is a Daytona model, which means that in 1963, it had an R2 V-8 motor and disc brakes. And it has the mechanical sliding rear roof."

We walked into his other yard.

I was in front with Amiot while Brian, Michael, Clair, Jordon, and Ben followed with their various cameras. I kept warning them to watch out for the "landmines" that were left by Amiot's large but friendly dog.

Barn-finding, after all, is not for clean freaks.

Amiot showed us a 1969 Chevelle that he would sell for $1,500. Then we came upon another car that got my attention—a 1954 Ford two-door Ranch Wagon. I explained to him that I still own a 1953 Ranch Wagon that I bought as a senior in high school. "This belonged to a guy who had a tow truck," he said. "He hauled cars he found along Route 66. When he died, he had some beauties, but this one became surplus. I'll take four hundred dollars for the whole car."

I noticed it had the "Ranch Wagon" emblems I have been searching for. I offered him $100 for the logos, but he said he would only sell the whole car, not just the emblems.

Of course as soon as Brian heard that the Lincoln was owned by a celebrity, he had to get involved. Here he is sitting in the right rear seat, exactly where Ella sat when she was chauffeured around Beverly Hills.

Ella Fitzgerald's license plate.

To prove the car's celebrity ownership, Amiot produced this registration card.

Up the street from Amiot's collection is Silva's Saloon, established in 1933 by Felix Silva, the day after Prohibition ended. Today Felix Silva Jr. runs the establishment.

Claire Walters, our colleague from Hagerty Insurance, said she had never been to a bar before, but the way she ordered up a drink from owner Felix Jr., made me think otherwise.

(At press time, I was still trying to convince him to sell me the emblems . . .)

We came across a Saab Sonnet—the more angular, second-generation model.

"I drove that car eighty-five miles per hour," he said. "Paid five hundred dollars for it. But then the master cylinder went out, so I just parked it."

The correct V-4 Ford industrial engine powered it and it had a four-speed on the column and correct alloy rims with red-striped tires. This one had a customized front end, so the headlights had been lowered into the grille. Still, it was a rare fiberglass sports car for sale for just $1,500.

I said I would take it if he would deliver it to my home in North Carolina. He said his nephew lives in Mooresville, just one town away from mine. I encouraged him to visit his nephew and bring the car to me.

Ben, from Hagerty, said that his first car was a 1974 Sonnet. Small world.

There were more vehicles—Lincolns, Mustangs, an interesting '66 Chevy pickup with a built-on camper. There were other '58 Chevys, a four-door hardtop, a '58 Biscayne two-door sedan, and another Studebaker Lark.

This was a worthwhile stop. We thanked Amiot, but before we left, Jordon and Ben asked if they could stay until after sunset in order to capture the amazing lighting against the pink mountains.

Before we left Amiot's, he showed us some concrete pavement on the rear of his property along the railroad tracks. "This was part of the original Route 66 from before World War II," he said. "I had to dig up a lot of it when I built these buildings and to run water and electrical lines underground. It's at least twelve inches thick."

What that meant was that the last couple of hours we had spent looking at old cars had been not near, but literally *on* the original Route 66.

Amiot suggested that before we leave town, we should visit Silva's Saloon, the oldest bar in New Mexico. How could we decline?

Silva's was opened in 1933 after Prohibition ended. Felix Silva Sr. owned it, and today his son, Felix Silva Jr., runs it. It has been featured in numerous magazine stories, TV documentaries, and movies.

"I've been coming here since I was six months old," said Felix Jr. "People have been just leaving stuff here from the beginning," which explains the huge amount of paraphernalia on the walls.

Felix Jr. said that the bar was selected by *Esquire* magazine in 2000 as one of the top five bars in America. So while we waited for Jordon and Ben to finish up their sunset video project, we enjoyed a couple of beers. It was a great way to end the day.

Onto our hotel in Albuquerque.

HELLO, TOM?

We were in Bernalillo, New Mexico, about to look at a 1961 Lincoln Continental that had once belonged to jazz singer extraordinaire Ella Fitzgerald when my cell phone rang.

The call was from my friend Mike McClelland. "Hello, Tom?" Mike said.

"Hi, Mike," I responded. "What's up?"

"You wouldn't happen to be in New Mexico, would you?" he asked.

That was surprising, because I didn't tell Mike that I was taking the Route 66 trip. "Yes, I am," I replied. "How did you know?"

"Well, I just passed a yellow 1939 Ford Woody, and I told my wife, 'I think that's Tom Cotter's car,'" he said. "She said, 'You've got to be kidding.'"

Mike and his wife, Vicki, live in Mooresville, North Carolina, less than 10 miles from my house in Davidson, but nearly 2,000 miles from Bernalillo. They own a number of collector cars, including an Auburn, a 1941 Packard, 1951 Ford, and an Austin Healey 3000. Mike is also a board member at the Auburn Cord Duesenberg Museum.

They had just flown from Charlotte to Albuquerque, New Mexico, to visit friends. They picked up their rental car and started to drive toward their friend's house, and that's when they saw my car.

"I would have bet a hundred dollars that when I called you, you were going to say, 'No, it's not me,'" Mike said.

But it was me.

Like two car guys passing in the night.

◆ WEDNESDAY, NOVEMBER 11, 2015 ◆

We knew exactly where we needed to be this morning—we had been told about the Lewis Auto and Toy Museum, just east of Albuquerque, by a number of people. But the museum opened at 9 a.m. and we were out early, so we decided to follow up on another lead first.

Jim Goodman (a friend of Michael's) had been following our Route 66 exploits on Facebook and gave Michael a hot tip. Goodman graduated from Pascack Hills High School, Class of '74, in Montvale, New Jersey, with Michael. They hadn't seen each other in forty years. Goodman sent a message to Michael saying that his friend had a salvage yard and a building with lots of old cars. Goodman's friend was named Jack Dautel, but everyone called him Boomer.

Boomer shared the collection with us that he and his father built over a thirty-year period.

AUTO SALVAGE HOT RODDER	CAR COUNT **37**	FOR SALE Yes ★ No Maybe

Boomer is in the auto salvage business. He's been in the business his whole life and so had his father. They were also both hot rodders and spent all their free time modifying old cars.

Boomer showed me his small tow truck collection that came from the original Route 66 Wreckers. "Up until 2004, they were on Route 66 forever," he said. "That's a 1965 and that's 1968. We still use them every day. Route 66 Wreckers used to run the Unser's Wrecking Yard for them."

Boomer was talking about the famous Unser racing family, Bobby, Al Sr., and Al Jr., all Indianapolis 500 and Pike Peak winners.

Michael's high school buddy Jim Goodman turned us onto his friend Jack "Boomer" Dautel's cool collection of barn-finds and old hot rods. Boomer makes his living in the towing and salvage business.

Boomer's 1959 Plymouth Fury really got my attention. Except for a cracked windshield, the car looks and drives great. He said that he uses the car as his daily driver when he's not driving a tow truck.

Boomer's 1953 Cadillac is a wonderful car that could be buffed and waxed and driven as-is. But these cars are Boomer's personal collection and are not for sale. Sorry.

Sprinkled throughout Boomer's yard was a unique collection of old cars. Boomer showed me a 1959 Plymouth Fury, which appeared to be in very good condition. "It has 88,000 miles on it now. I drive it all the time," he said. "It's one year newer than the car in the movie *Christine*, which was a 1958. It has a Polyspheric Semi-Hemi V-8 with a pushbutton Torqueflite transmission," Boomer said. "I need a new windshield, but they are five hundred dollars. So, for the time being, I'll drive with the cracked one."

I noticed a number of 1955 through '57 Chevys. "Yeah, I have quite a few Tri-five Chevys," he said. I noted a 1955 Chevy passenger car pickup, like an early El Camino. Boomer told me it had been cut down from a sedan delivery back in 1962. Unique, but sad that a sought-after model had been chopped up.

I asked Boomer if it was for sale. "No, pretty much everything back here is my stash," he said. "Nothing's for sale."

We walked past a few Model A Fords, a 1928 coupe and a 1931 roadster, a nice old Cadillac, two neat old Ford trucks. We walked into the building where Boomer and his father had built street rods.

Wow.

Outside his shop, Boomer stored a bunch of interesting future projects, such as this 1936 Ford five-window coupe. He intends to go back into the street rod business, so cars like this might be resurrected again.

Boomer's four-month wonder; after retrieving a Deuce body in Missouri, he completed this tribute to *American Grafitti* hot rod in just four month's time.

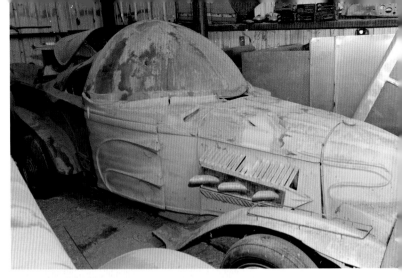

When we walked into Boomer's shop, cars were covered and dusty, seemingly untouched for years. Before his father passed away, Boomer and his dad would build hot rods in this building together.

Would you believe this started out as a 1932 Ford roadster pickup? Built by a local customizer in the 1950s, this unfinished Hemi-powered radical custom was fabricated totally of metal and lead, no Bondo.

It was cluttered and dusty, but loaded with jaw-dropping stuff. He first showed us a bright yellow '32 Ford five-window, a dead ringer to the *American Graffiti* hot rod. Boomer said he bought the body in Missouri and had the car completed from scratch in four months. I commented that I could write an entire book about his garage. Most of the cars had been in the building for at least fourteen years. "I was in the street rod business for twenty years," he said. "But there is more money in towing and salvage."

He showed us a 1927 Chrysler with a 500-cubic-inch Cadillac engine installed. He said it couldn't get traction, so he installed huge rear tires and stretched the rear fenders to 18 inches wide.

Boomer showed us a crazy-looking custom that he said started out as a 1932 Ford roadster pickup. The man who created it died in 1976 before he could finish the project, so Boomer and his father pieced it back together. "All that work was done in lead," he said. "It's all steel that was filled in with lead. It has a Chrysler Firedome Hemi engine in it."

I had to admit to Boomer that I admire all the hard work the creator put into the car, but I thought it was ugly. Boomer said it looks better outside and cleaned up.

"The bubble windshield came out of the Arizona aircraft graveyard," he said. "It's right out of the sixties Ed Roth, George Barris era."

Then he showed us a 1936 Chevy pickup, the car his father was working on when he became ill. "It has a GM-tuned port-injection engine in it," he said. "We were some of the first guys in the country putting these engines in hot rods. It runs and drives perfectly."

He told us he knows where stashes of trucks like this are in Kansas. Could have used that info a week earlier!

A 1959 Chevy Impala, a nice original car with a 283, belongs to his little sister. But the car that got our attention was a 1951 Mercury two-door. "It has ninety thousand miles on it," he said. "My dad had it painted Candy Apple, but it's all original. This is another car we were working on when he got sick."

Boomer told us he is going to move his salvage and towing business to another building a few miles away because an interstate highway is going to come through his property. "The building I'm buying has a shop and a showroom, so I'll be able to put all these cars on display," he said. "It's an old Chevy dealership that closed in the eighties. I'll run the towing service and a street rod shop out of there."

We kept walking through the cluttered building. "This is a 1955 Ford Victoria with a 1956 312 engine in it," he said. "It runs and drives and is basically original."

And yet another 1957 Chevy with a tuned port engine and a 700R transmission. Then we came upon a 1936 Ford Tudor sedan.

"That one took third in the World of Wheels," he said. "It has a built-to-the-max 350 and beat a twelve-second car on the street once. It has a B&M turbo."

I noticed another yard of old cars just a couple of hundred feet from Boomer's. I walked over, but nobody was there. I asked Boomer about it and he said he would call the owner for us.

Just before departing for the Lewis Auto and Toy Museum, Brian got a call that he was needed back home in North Carolina to deal with family business. So we dropped him off at the airport and reluctantly said goodbye. It would be tough to be both driver and navigator in the Woody while still looking for

This 1951 Mercury is one of the rare, never-been-chopped coupes. Boomer'sfather had the car painted in Candy Apple, but it remains flathead powered.

The same customizer who built the radical '32 Ford also built this 1955 Chevy El Camino, converting it from a sedan delivery. Boomer had another one just like it outside.

old cars for the rest of New Mexico, Arizona, and California. But somehow we'd make it work.

When Michael was finished shooting inside the building, we said goodbye to Boomer and started to head east toward the museum in Moriarty, New Mexico.

GREAT STUFF, NONE FOR SALE

CAR COUNT 700

FOR SALE ☐ Yes ★ No ☐ Maybe

Archie Lewis, with his ponytail, is the coolest eighty-year-old I ever met. He doesn't sell anything, but enjoys talking with people when they come to look over his collection.

Archie Lewis made it clear up front that nothing in his collection was for sale. Still, an 8-acre yard with seven hundred cars along the interstate was something we had to inspect.

The outside lot had hundreds of rusty relics, both trucks and cars. Some were restorable and others would be better used as parts cars or yard sculpture. "I moved here from Albuquerque about twelve years ago, but I've been in business for many years," said the eighty-year-old. "I started collecting cars sixty years ago."

We had heard so much about Archie Lewis's museum in Moriarty, New Mexico. He has been collecting cars for sixty years. Inside he kept his primo cars, those he restored or nice original models.

Lewis still owns the Model T touring car that he bought for $30 when he was nine. Many of the cars Lewis owns were retrieved on the way to being scrapped. "I was in the old car parts business from 1954 until I moved out here," he said. "I sold reproduction parts for Model T, Model A, and V-8 Fords. When I moved here, I had to tow seven hundred cars. I had help, but it took me seven months. I'm kind of picky; I don't buy every old car I find. See that Thunderbird? I bought it brand new. Now it has a 427 in it. It has about eighty thousand miles on it, but hasn't run in probably thirty years."

Lewis bought this 1957 Thunderbird new and eventually installed a 427 side-oiler engine in place of the original 312. But sadly, he admits he hasn't driven it in thirty years.

Of the seven hundred cars that Lewis had on site, this Cabover tanker truck hit my hot button. Hopefully one day this solid New Mexico truck will receive a full restoration.

I have not seen fields of cars like this since I was a kid reading *Rod & Custom* magazines. But this scene is not forty years old; it was taken during our trip down Route 66 in the fall of 2015.

He told me that in the other part of his building he had lots of his old tools and parts in addition to an original Model T, Model A, and a 1935 Ford.

When we had seen everything at the Lewis Auto and Toy Museum, we began heading west again, back toward Boomer's yard. So far, this had been an amazing morning; we met a couple of characters and found a *huge* volume of cars, all before lunchtime!

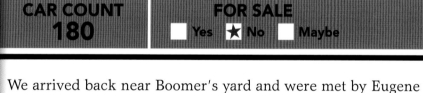

MISTEE'S ECLECTIC COLLECTION

CAR COUNT	FOR SALE		
180	Yes	★ No	Maybe

We arrived back near Boomer's yard and were met by Eugene Burditt, who ran the old scrapyard for owner Mistee Thomson.

The cars in this yard had been here for a long, long time. Some were restorable—most were parts cars. They were all interesting, though, especially the one with the tree growing through it.

Even though Mistee Thomson doesn't come to his yard every day, employee Eugene Burditt allowed us to photograph every corner of his long-closed salvage yard.

We visited this yard on Veterans Day, so Thomson was celebrating at the Veterans Day parade and wouldn't be joining us. But we appreciated him allowing us to walk through his yard with our notepads, cameras, and video recorders.

"This place has been in business since 1972," said our guide, Burditt. "It was originally set up as a towing and storage yard by Dugger's Towing Service. When the partners all went their separate ways, Mistee wound up with the place. He had been collecting cars since he was eighteen years old."

As we walked around, I saw a variety of cars: a 1941 Chrysler convertible, a couple of Ford Counsels, a few Crosleys. "Mistee has groups of Cadillacs, Hudsons, even a group of old GM Flexible buses in the back," he said.

Luxury Cars Only! Mistee's has this row of premium cars: a 1947 Cadillac, what I believe is a 1936 Caddy, and a 1955 Packard. The yard had rows of common-make cars, Lincolns, Crosleys, and more.

What a sad sight. This 1936 Ford Fordor sedan could be a wonderful project for someone, but instead it has sat in the open for decades. Nothing in the yard is for sale, by the way.

Do you think this car has been parked there for a while? This car not only has a tree poking through the windshield and roof, but it also winds its way through the steering wheel! Obviously, Mistee's has been a salvage yard for a long time.

There was a 1924 Model T coupe, which hot rodders call a phone booth coupe. "That's a tall-cab coupe and has been sitting there for as long as I have known him," Burditt said.

As I was walking with Burditt, something caught my attention and I had to stop. It was a 1950 Ford sedan and next to it was the nose of a Crosley. The design was almost identical, except of course the Crosley was scaled down. I had never seen them together before, and they certainly made an interesting comparison.

Burditt showed us a 1933 travel trailer. It was the oldest I'd ever seen. Next, in the middle of the yard was a large old building. Burditt explained to us that it was built in 1900 as a railroad building, where engineers and conductors slept during long hauls.

Crawling through the yard was certainly a chore, with trees and plant growth up to 5 feet tall. We came upon a 1929 Model A Ford that yard owner Mistee actually drove in high school. I'm not sure how cars could ever be removed from the rear of this yard, unless a helicopter could be utilized. This place was crowded, yet Burditt said they once cleared out 175 cars from here!

We climbed inside some of the old GM buses on the rear of the property. Burditt said

Left: Mistee's had several of these General Motors Flexible buses. A couple of them were complete and restorable, except without drivetrains. If these buses could talk, imagine the stories they could tell about driving on Route 66 from Chicago to LA in the 1940s and '50s. Right: It is amazing that the interiors in these seventy-five-year-old buses are still in good condition, complete with seats and luggage racks. One of the buses at Mistee's had been converted to a motorhome.

Two noses: This is an amazing comparison—a 1950 Ford and a similar year Crosley. Look at how similar the styling is, albeit at different scales.

the buses were probably built in 1939 or 1940. They were very much intact, with interior seating, book racks, and grab rails. It made me wonder how many people traveled Route 66 in buses just like these, seeking a new life in the West.

Walking toward the front, we passed a couple of Saab 96 station wagons, a Rover 2000TC, and an RX2 Mazda. These are cars we don't find very often.

Burditt had spent a lot of time trudging through the overgrown yard with us. We told him thanks and hit the road toward Gallup, the last bigger city before we crossed the Arizona state line.

We stayed on old Route 66 when we could—going through towns such as Grant and Milan—but because the sun was going down earlier, we jumped on the interstate once it got dark for the final dash into Gallup.

Out here in the desert there is nothing. *Nothing*. We drove for miles and miles before seeing any signs of life: a home, a gas station. I'm sure there were cars out there, but it might require an airplane or a helicopter to access them.

◆ EL RANCHO HOTEL ◆

Claire, our Hagerty colleague, made hotel reservations for us in one of the classic Route 66 hotels—El Rancho. This was to be the most memorable evening of our trip.

El Rancho was an amazing place. It was built in 1936 especially for Hollywood actors who needed a place to call home while they were shooting Westerns in the desert. The hotel has terrific neon signs and an amazing lobby. Each room is named after a movie star who stayed in it. I stayed in the Denis Morgan room, next to the Susan Haywood room and across the hall from the Fred MacMurray room.

As I walked from my room toward the stairs that led to the lobby, I passed Betty Grable's and Jimmy Stewart's old rooms. I read that other

frequent guests included Ronald Reagan, Spencer Tracy, Katherine Hepburn, and Kirk Douglas. El Rancho's lobby is adorned with autographed photos. I would definitely stay there again and would recommend it to anyone seeking an authentic Route 66 experience.

During our dinner in the bar area of El Rancho, we sat next to some members of the motorcycle gang, the Bandidos. They wore all the black leather jackets and boots. They looked menacing, but seemed like pretty good guys.

We told them we were looking for old cars and they gave us a tip about a junkyard we could follow up on the next morning. "Go on the road between the Home Depot and the Walmart," one of them said. "When the road turns to gravel, turn right and go to that junkyard."

This was a great way to conclude one heck of a productive car-finding day. And those Bandidos?

Real nice guys!

The Bandidos may look menacing, but they're pretty good guys.

BANDIDOS BARN-FIND BLOWOUT

CAR COUNT	FOR SALE		
40	★ Yes	No	Maybe

We woke up early because all of us were still in an Eastern time zone mindset. After a breakfast at El Rancho, we took off to find the Walmart and Home Depot. We needed to cover some miles today because we had to be at the Santa Monica Pier by Sunday afternoon, which was only three days away. But we easily

David Giron was a great tour guide, car enthusiast, and salvage yard manager. He was personally interested in acquiring two cars, the Toyota FJ and an Austin-Healey Sprite, as personal projects.

We found so many trucks on this trip, especially Chevy trucks like this. So many, in fact, that I could probably write a barn-find truck book! ABQ Auto Salvage certainly had a number of them hidden in the weeds.

How many rat rodders would love to have this authentic paint scheme on their ride? If the recent graffiti additions on this '55 Ford could be removed, it could be a hit at the next cars and coffee.

found the Home Depot and the Walmart a few miles away and, within a few minutes, found the junkyard the Bandidos had mentioned.

We met David Giron, manager of ABQ Auto Salvage and Recycling in Gallup, New Mexico. Giron said they did indeed have some old cars in the back, but they hadn't mowed the weeds there in a long time, so it might be tough going.

We told him we were into the adventure, so we all trudged back there to see what they had. As we were walking toward the rear of the property, Giron told me that everything was for sale. That was good news, since we saw almost one thousand cars the day before and none were for sale.

"I've worked here since we opened four years ago," he said. "But I worked in the owner's other yard in Albuquerque since I was sixteen. I'm twenty-five now. We got a lot of these cars from a man who used to collect old cars, but he died. We had more than one hundred, but we sold many of those."

We first came upon a 1953 Ford pickup that had a solid body. We kept walking through the desert-type landscape toward the old car section. I asked Giron if there were rattlesnakes around here.

"Yes, many," he said. "But they are all asleep for the winter."

My favorite in the ABQ yard was certainly this Packard taxi, which I believe was a 1947. The car was most definitely a taxi and had holes in the roof where the sign once mounted.

Jordon was filming me "getting dirty" at the ABQ Auto Salvage yard. It was hard getting near some of the cars and identifying them. If it was summer and the snakes were out, I don't think I would have jumped into this quagmire.

What a relief! Thankfully, we didn't make this trip in July or we might have needed to use that snake-bite kit Michael recommended.

We looked at a 1946 or '47 Packard Clipper taxi that seemed to be authentic. It was painted yellow and had the taxi markings and the holes in the roof where a sign would have mounted. We all agreed it was our favorite find of the day so far—of course, it was only 9 a.m.

Giron told us that they stopped showing these old cars because people would come back at night and steal parts. "Maybe it was the Bandidos gang," he said with a laugh. "That's how they knew there were old cars back here."

Dodges, Chevys, and Fords were lined up neatly but surrounded by huge weeds. If this had been in the East, I would have worried about Lyme disease from ticks. Here was a 1954 Ford Sedan Delivery, which is a rare and desirable car, and a fire truck and tow truck. This place certainly had a diverse inventory.

In the old car lineup was an FJ Toyota that appeared to have solid project potential. A onceover showed that it had zero rust. I'd say it could be restored with the original six-cylinder engine or hot-rodded with a Chevy V-8, like the conversions that Icon Vehicle Dynamics perform on $100,000-plus models.

Giron really likes this Toyota, but he would sell it. I asked if he would take $3,000 for it. "I would probably take five thousand," he said.

Similar to the FJ, we came across a couple of Jeep Grand Wagoneers—you know the ones with the fake wood siding. These vehicles, even though

I explained to Jordon while he was filming about the significance of crushing this 1992 Chevy Lumina. Fun, but also sad, that this once useful car that costs thousands of dollars new was salvaged for about $100 and now was going to be ground up for scrap.

Nuevo Classic: ABQ manager David Giron said he would sell this Jeep Grand Wagoneer for $2,500. I think that is a decent buy for a western car that was still complete. These cars have become modern-day Woodies in high-end resort towns.

they get outrageously poor fuel mileage, have quite a following among the resort crowd in areas such as Aspen or Cape Cod. There is even a business in Texas called Wagonmasters that buys, sells, and restores these vehicles.

"We won't sell parts off these Wagoneers," Giron said. "We will only sell the whole cars. We would probably sell this car for twenty five hundred dollars. The other one has no engine and would sell for less, probably fifteen hundred."

I asked Giron how much cars are scrapping for these days. "Really, really low," he said. "I don't want to tell you. I would say we would give one hundred fifty dollars for a complete car. The Chinese are not buying metal from America right now."

Then he asked us a helluva question. "Would you like to crush a car? Is the Pope Catholic? Of course I would!

This was a once-in-a-lifetime opportunity. He gave me the chance to push the button on the car crusher machine to flatten an early '90s Chevy Lumina. It was a blast.

Prior to this, the coolest industrial-type machines I had operated was driving the Grave Digger monster truck about 100 feet, and steering the S.S. *Badger* ferry boat across late Michigan. Notch another one to my bucket list!

We heard about a street rod shop on the east side of town called Ted's Street Rods. We found the shop and met Ted Gonzales, a hot rodder to the bone. Ted said his wife, Linda, would be arriving shortly.

Two of the coolest people we met on the trip, Ted and Linda Gonzales are hot rodders through and through, and often are Good Samaritans to old car enthusiasts who break down on Route 66 near Gallup, New Mexico.

LINDA WANTS TO BURN RUBBER!

CAR COUNT	FOR SALE		
14	☐ Yes	★ No	☐ Maybe

"Being we're in the Yellow Pages, and I'm the New Mexico representative for the National Street Rod Association, we have met and helped so many people who are driving their old cars on Route 66," Gonzales told us.

Gonzales had a few old cars outside his building—some were customers' cars and some were his. One odd combination was a 1930

Ted Gonzales's daily driver is this 1957 Ford Ranch Wagon, a solid two-door wagon with a 302 engine.

Model A sedan with a 1940 Mercury fender just resting on the front of it. It looked funky, but I liked it. Ted drives a 1957 Ford Ranch Wagon as his daily driver—another funky car, and one I *really* liked.

Inside the building he showed us Linda's pickup project—a 1940 Ford. He had just completed the chassis. He's about to install a tunnel port Chevy 350 from a police car that only has 30,000 miles. "Linda doesn't care what engine I put in it, as long as it burns rubber," he said.

Linda sounded like the ideal car wife. I couldn't wait to meet her.

On the other side of the shop, he showed us a 1950 Mercury coupe that his father and he started to build years ago. It was reminiscent of James Dean's car from *Rebel Without a Cause*.

"Dad wasn't a hot rodder, but he was a thinker," Gonzales said. "We didn't know how to chop a top, but the two of us learned how to do it on this

Ted is building this 1940 Ford pickup truck for his wife, Linda. Linda is a pickup truck version of Mustang Sally; she really doesn't care about what year or make the body is, or what drivetrain powers it, only that it burns rubber!

I don't know why I was attracted to this, a Model A Tudor with a 1940 Mercury fender resting on it. This car is not being built with the Merc fender, but I thought it looked pretty cool.

The chopped-top Merc that Ted and his father started to build many years ago. The suspension and drivetrain is in place, but it needs lots of exterior and interior finishing.

Ted and Linda have this 1949 Ford Business Coupe, which is totally bitchin'. The business coupes were built for salesmen to haul their various samples and catalogs in, so they had no back seat.

car. My dad came out here on a horse and buggy, worked for the railroad, and died at ninety-eight years old. We also built a '32 Ford roadster together."

Ted's wife, Linda, walked into the shop. From what her husband told me, this was one cool lady. We spoke to Linda about her project pickup Ted was building—I asked her, "What do you want in a hot rod?"

"I want to be able to burn rubber," she said. "Actually he originally gave me a 1937 Dodge pickup for Valentine's Day. Only Ted could get away with something like that. My friends just didn't understand. I've been into hot rods since I married Ted thirty-two years ago. I was into fast cars before I met Ted, but then I met Ted and changed to hot rods."

The other car the Gonzaleses have parked at their house is this 1955 Ford Crown Victoria. This car belonged to Ted's high school friend Herman, who was tragically killed in a motorcycle wreck.

Ted realized the '55 Ford had been his friend Herman's car decades earlier because of the way Herman painted the hubcaps, which amazingly were still mounted on the car.

Ted and Linda told us about an old car that was on a nearby Indian reservation years ago. "The man said he had a Deusenberry," Gonzales said. "I said, 'Do you mean a Duesenberg?'

"He said, 'No, it was a Deusenberry,' but when I started to ask about what color the engine was, and they said green, and it had pipes that came out the sides of the hood, I realized what it was. I missed that one, though. They said some white men bought it."

Ted said he once saw an aluminum 1932 Lincoln that was taken from a reservation. Another was a Cadillac Biarritz. "You've got to remember that this was Route 66," he said. "So when cars broke down, they were just left in town and the Indians could buy them cheap. Some of them are still out there. We used to be able to drive around the reservations on a Sunday afternoon and look for cool cars, but it's harder now. The easy-to-find cars have been bought up, so now you have to go deeper into the reservations to find anything."

Gonzales offered to take us to his house where he had a couple of other old cars. One was a 1955 Ford Crown Victoria. "That Ford belonged to a friend of mine, Herman, who drove it in high school," he said. "Herman was killed in a motorcycle wreck right after high school, but he had this 1955 Ford Crown Vic. It went through several owners, but I bought it because I knew it was his because of the way he painted the spinner hubcaps."

Gonzales saw an ad for the 1955 Ford seven years ago. The people who were selling it wanted $5,000, but after he told them the story about Herman, they reduced the price to $2,500. The car today still retains the stock 292-cubic-inch and three-speed gearbox.

He showed us another car in his yard, a 1949 Ford Business Coupe. This is a rare car because it has no back seat. "It still has the flathead and runs well," he said. "I bought it in Albuquerque and drove it back here. I'll probably install 302s in both the '55 and the '49," he said.

HOLY ROLLER MUSCLE MONSTER

CAR COUNT
1

FOR SALE
★ Yes ☐ No ☐ Maybe

Father Matt Keller built a hot Chevelle in high school, and now turning fifty years old, wanted to build another one. He employed volunteers, students, and even other priests and the bishop to assist in the project.

We followed Gonzales to the local Catholic Church. He said there was a car there I needed to see. It was just a couple of blocks from Ted and Linda's home.

Ted introduced us to Father Matt Keller of the Sacred Heart Cathedral, who, with the assistance of volunteers like Ted, is restoring a big-block 1972 Chevelle. "I've been a hot rodder since I was a kid," Father Keller said. "When I was fifteen, I dragged home a 1964 Malibu SuperSport that I bought for twelve hundred dollars. It was in primer and it was a mess. I took vo-tech courses in high school, so I did all the bodywork, and my buddy built the engine and my brother was a painter. So by the time I was a senior in high school, I had this really sweet Malibu S/S."

Father Keller regrets selling the car when he went off to college. "Worst mistake I ever made," he said. "There is nothing I learned in college that I would rather have than that Chevelle."

Father Keller explained that the car we were looking at, the 1972 Chevelle, was a fundraising tool for the church's vocational program. "It takes quite a bit of money to go to seminary and become a priest," he said. "Basically it's as expensive as getting a master's degree. So I decided to use the interest and skills that God gave me to try to raise money for the program."

He bought a 1972 Chevelle donor car and went about restoring it from the

This amazing restoration is taking place not in a traditional shop, but in a Catholic Church parish! Proceeds from the sale of the completed big-block 1972 Chevelle SS will help offset expenses for new seminarians.

Father Keller was so pleased with the powder coating he performed in the garage in a thrift shop oven. He powder-coated the wheels, springs, upper-control arms, door hinges, and anything else that would fit in the oven.

frame up. Keller is doing the powder coating on suspension components himself using an oven he purchased for $40 in the thrift store.

"People from the community who come to help us on the car won't necessarily come in the front doors of the church. So it's an evangelization and community builder as well. It's just great. We had a retreat here this summer for young men interested in the priesthood, and we timed it when the body was ready to go back on. So these guys lifted the body back on the chassis. Even the bishop was here that day and helped us lift the body onto the chassis. We're going to paint it the priestly colors, black body with white stripes and a white interior," he said. "The car will have a built 454 four-speed, twelve-bolt posi unit. We had to put floorpans in and we put on new rear quarter panels."

Keller said that on nice days like the day we visited, he pushes the car into the driveway and it almost starts accidents when people pass by. Keller said the building just used to be the parish garage, but now it's a shop, equipped with tools, compressors, and welders.

"People come and help, and I'm able to hear their confessions right out here in the shop," he said. "I come out here every day, wearing my black coveralls. People look at my hands and ask if I'm going to serve communion with those hands."

I asked what project he might tackle after this one is completed. "A muscle car is just great because everyone is interested in them and you can get all the parts off the Internet," he said. "It's just a great platform. I would like to do this again. We planned to complete this restoration in one year, which has been pretty demanding. So if we do another restoration, we'll either buy a better car or make it a couple-of-year project and take the time pressure off us."

Last winter Father Keller said he spent out in the garage, freezing and drilling out all the spot-welds that hold the quarter panels to the car.

Father Keller said that last year, facing fifty years old and a midlife crisis, he began searching for the Chevelle he drove in high school, which he sold in his early twenties.

"But I couldn't find anything with the VIN number on it," he said, "and the insurance company had destroyed all their old paper records. This car is a better project than finding my old car because it's not so personal."

He told us we were in a part of the world where there are still a lot of old cars in good shape. On every car-finding trip, I find a favorite car, a favorite person, a favorite story. This one is, without a doubt, the best old car story I have ever heard. Perhaps it's because I am a Catholic and teach in a Catholic college, but I had tears in my eyes after hearing Father Keller's story. It was a great day.

Before we left Father Keller's "shop," Ted Gonzales suggested we look for a bunch of old cars on the Arizona state line. "It's right next to the Rest Area," he said. "You can't miss it."

But we did miss it. Drove right by it and didn't realize it until we were past the exit. So we drove to the next exit, thankfully not far, and doubled back. I'm glad we did, not only because it was a cool story, but also because several days later, I'd be back there needing help.

Alvin Yellowhorse

NAVAJO BARN-FINDER

CAR COUNT	FOR SALE		
19	★ Yes	No	Maybe

We met with the owner of the old cars, Alvin Yellowhorse. Yellowhorse is an entrepreneur, owning all the old cars, a repair shop, but also a jewelry design business.

"The old cars are my hobby; I make jewelry for a living," Yellowhorse said. "I've been hunting old cars for probably twelve years. I bring these cars in from all over the reservation."

I didn't know it, but we were on Navajo land. We were standing right next to a huge mountain he called Blasting Rock. He said it is where all the rock came from for the railroads that were built in the 1800s. "I drive around in my truck and look for old cars," he said. "If they are not for sale, I don't bother them, but if they are, I buy them."

Below this amazing mountain, called Blasting Rock, Alvin Yellowhorse stores his old cars just west of Gallup, New Mexico. These two cars were dragged out of a gully, where decades of occasional heavy rain had them partially buried.

I asked Yellowhorse if he is able to secure titles when he buys these cars. "Sometime I get titles, but most of the time it was grandpa's truck that has just been sitting in the yard," he said. "No titles around, sometimes. I collect them, but I sell them also. Everything back here is for sale."

When we met him, he had just picked up a 1948 Plymouth Special Deluxe from Prescott, Arizona. He said it runs, but he didn't have a battery to start it. "The floorboards are shot, but someone bought new floorboards already, so it comes with those. I'm asking sixty five hundred dollars for it."

Some of the other reservation finds include a 1936 Ford and a 1951 Chevy that he literally dug out of a gully. "I've got a couple of others I'm going to dig

Yellowhorse recently dragged home this '48 Plymouth, which is partially restored. He is asking $6,500 for it.

There is no shortage of surface-rusted trucks in the New Mexico desert. But underneath that patina is usually a solid body and floorpans. Everything that Yellowhorse has is for sale.

A solid old Caddy project, waiting for an enthusiastic new owner! Most of the cars that Yellowhorse acquires are from nearby reservations. His cars are stored on a Navajo Reservation on the state line between Arizona and New Mexico.

out of gullies one of these days, a Model T and something else that I can't identify because it is upside-down."

We walked around his property and looked at several cars and trucks. His favorite is the old 1949 Chevy truck that runs and drives. "Everyone knows me here," he said. "And I've been handing out cards for years, so people call me."

I was intrigued with a project pickup that Yellowhorse was working on. It was a 1937 GMC that he is chopping the top on. He plans to make it a rat rod but have it ride on a newer S10 frame. "Chopping a top is tougher than it seems," he says.

As the sun started to set, Yellowhorse's wife and daughters stopped by to visit him. They were a terrific family. I even met the family dog, Dutch.

We said goodbye to Yellowhorse, not knowing that it wouldn't be the last time. Until we meet again, Dutch!

CHAPTER 7

ROUTE 66

ARIZONA

We hightailed it out of New Mexico and into Arizona, after sunset. We stayed on I-40 all the way to Flagstaff because, well, there's precious little of Route 66 *at* all in the eastern half of the state. Except for small sections of extremely rough pavement, hardly any of old Route 66 is worth traveling on east of Flagstaff.

. . . .

But we did stop in Winslow, Arizona, for a photograph at a certain street corner made famous in the 1972 song by Jackson Browne and later recorded by the Eagles. And then we blasted through the night at speeds up to 80 miles per hour toward our waiting hotel in Flagstaff.

The old Woody was working harder than probably at any time in its seventy-six-year-old life. I have an experienced and trained ear when it comes to my cars, and I started to hear a new noise I had not heard before. After stopping for fuel, I stuck my head underneath the Woody to see where the noise might be coming from, but because it was dark, I couldn't figure it out. I figured it might have been a broken exhaust gasket either where the headers bolt to the cylinder heads or where the headers attach to the exhaust system.

Anyway, I certainly couldn't solve it on a cold evening in the dark—I'd have to look into it in the morning. So I kept on driving toward Flagstaff, new noise be damned!

Get Your Kicks

ARIZONA
66
ALL AMERICAN ROAD

Welcome
— to —
Arizona's Historic
Route 66

Presented By

HISTORIC ROUTE 66
ARIZONA
66
ALL AMERICAN ROAD

Historic Route 66
Association of Arizona
120 W. Andy Devine Ave. (PO Box 66)
Kingman, Arizona 86402
928-753-5001
azrt66.com

"I was standing on a corner in Winslow, Arizona" . . .
are the lyrics of the song "Take It Easy," written and
performed by both Jackson Browne and the Eagles. Notice
the flatbed Ford in the background. We had to stop there!

Some of the historic gas stations along Route 66 are beautifully
restored and are operating as tourist attractions. Others, like this
one, are sadly in disrepair and ignored.

We checked into a nice hotel rather late and found a restaurant that would serve us dinner. It was a tiring day—we had found a bunch of cars plus had driven more than 200 miles—so we were looking forward to getting some sleep.

◆ FRIDAY, NOVEMBER 13, 2015 ◆

I've been to Arizona many times over the past thirty years. I made numerous trips to Arizona International Speedway when I worked in the racing industry, made a few trips to the Grand Canyon, and produced a number of automotive new-car launches for BMW and Mercedes-Benz, mostly in the Scottsdale area. And I've been to Flagstaff twice, but I've never driven across the northern portion of the state before.

I was looking forward to it, if for no other reason than to visit Kingman, Arizona. That's where Ford Motor Company's secret test track was located and I wanted to visit. I became familiar with the test track while writing my first book, which was about the legendary race team, Holman-Moody.

Ex-Ford racing director, Jacques Passino, told me that Ford tested the GT40s, MK IIs, and MR IVs at the Kingman track before dominating the 24 Hours of LeMans races in 1966 and 1967. Passino told me that they ran forty-eight-hour tests with the cars at race speeds on the Kingman test track, figuring that if the cars could survive forty-eight hours of supervised testing, that they could survive twenty-four hours under racing conditions. So visiting Kingman has been on my bucket list for the past twenty five years.

I got up early Friday morning and drove the Woody around town to find a muffler and exhaust repair shop. It was early—6:30 a.m. or so—and I decided explore for old cars while I was waiting for repair shops to open. I spent about ninety minutes and found almost nothing. I figured that rather than spend more time in the Flagstaff area, we should keep heading west.

I stumbled upon Muffler Magic, right on Route 66. The man who worked there said he was totally booked up that day, and if it was a serious problem, he couldn't fix it until the next day. My heart started to race—we

needed to be in Santa Monica Sunday so that I could be back in Chicago at the end of the following week.

"I'll just put it on the lift and see what it is," he said. I drove the Woody onto the lift and he inspected the system from front to back on each side. Then he found the problem.

"Your exhaust hanger ripped off the pipe," he said. "It needs to be welded." I got real nervous, thinking that welding would be one of the major repairs he couldn't do.

"It won't be a problem," he said. "I'll have it fixed in a few minutes." Whew!

Thirty-five dollars later I was back on the road toward the hotel to meet my traveling companions with a quiet Woody, ready to hit the road. We had two and a half days remaining. Route 66 begins again just west of Flagstaff and becomes an absolutely terrific and scenic alternative to I-40. Once we got off I-40 and back onto Route 66, we passed a series of the nostalgic Burma-Shave signs along the road. Below is a selection of those signs—at least the ones I could write down as I was driving past at 60 miles per hour!

If hugging highways
Is your sport
Trade your car
For a Davenport
Burma-Shave

Cattle crossing
Means go slow
That big old bull
Is some cow's beau
Burma-Shave

If daisies are
Your favorite flower
Keep pushing up
Your miles per hour
Burma-Shave

You can drive
A mile a minute
But there is no
Future in it
Burma-Shave

We passed though Seligman, Arizona, soon after rejoining Route 66. We had been told by a number of people along the way that there were lots of old cars in Seligman.

"Make sure you don't miss it," we were told.

Well, I don't recommend traveling to Seligman to look for old cars. The town is a tourist trap, and yes, a number of rusty old cars can be found up and down Main Street, but they are simply "props" to lure tourists into various stores—not really intended as automotive esoterica at all. Seligman reminded me of Myrtle Beach, South Carolina, or the Jersey Shore, except with a Wild West theme.

Another town we passed through on the old Route 66 was Peach Springs, which was, I am told, the model for the fictional Radiator Springs in the movie *Cars*.

In a little "wide spot in the road," called Truxton, Arizona, we stopped because we noticed a couple of cars behind a fence at a closed gas station.

The metropolis of Truxton has a population of about 250 people.

SECOND-GEN GEARHEAD	CAR COUNT 7	FOR SALE ★ Yes No Maybe

We pulled in and met owner Mike Sudberry, whose father started the station years ago and Mike ran until he retired in 2014.

Sudberry was a car guy; we spoke the same language. "My family moved here in 1970 from California and opened this garage," Sudberry said. "I closed down the business about a year ago. I'm doing my own thing now, restoring cars. Right now I'm working on a 1968 Dodge Charger."

He walked us to the side of the building where his old cars were stashed. The first vehicle we approached was a 1938 Ford

This '49 Olds 88 would make an ideal hot rod or rat rod. The body and floors, always the bane of East Coast restorers, were amazing on this car and most of the others Sudberry had on hand.

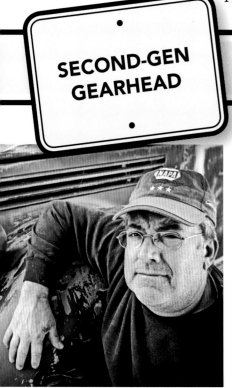

Mike Sudberry's father ran the fuel station until I-40 was completed and Route 66 became redundant. Then they began repairing cars.

We pulled into one of those closed stations because a bunch of old cars were parked behind a fence. We met owner Mike Sudberry, who had recently closed the station, and now buys, sells, and restores old cars.

This Studebaker will become a copy of one his father used to drag race in California back in the 1950s. It is one of several Studebakers that Sudberry and his father owned and sold over the past few years.

pickup. "That truck probably came off the same assembly line as my '39 Woody, but one year earlier," I told Sudberry.

"This is an unmolested 1938 Ford truck with almost no rust," he said. "Someone put an Offenhauser manifold on it years ago, but that's about it. I bought it with a spare engine and transmission, which are in the back of the truck. I spent a little bit of time getting all the doors and windows working. I put new tires on the rear and new tubes all around."

Sudbury bought it from a neighbor. "The guy had it laying around, and I tried to buy it for two or three years before he finally let it go."

I asked him if it was for sale. Sudberry said *everything* was for sale. "I'd like to get five thousand dollars for it," he said. "I think it's worth it, because it's never been messed with."

(I really liked this truck and thought about it for the rest of my trip. The latest trend in the old car world is to have trucks and cars with ugly paint jobs and reliable drivetrains. Most hot rodders work hard to add patina to their paint jobs. This truck, however, has authentic rough paint and patina. Don't be surprised if by the time you read this, that truck is in my garage!)

On to the next car—a 1951 Studebaker Starlight Coupe. "My father used to drag race one like this when he was in high school," he said. "It had the 259 cubic-inch Studebaker V-8 and a three-speed with overdrive. He said he could beat anything on the track except the

The car I fell in love with was this 1938 Ford pickup truck. I loved the natural patina. Don't be surprised if I own this truck by the time this book is published. The asking price of $5,000 was more than fair.

wide-track Oldsmobile, who would smoke Dad at the end of the day when the Studebaker was getting hot. My father bought this one in California a long time ago. He had always hoped to one day build one like he had in high school, but he never got it done before he passed away." Sudberry told me he would like to restore it in his father's memory one day.

So is it for sale?

"I'd price it for the 'I really don't want to sell it' price of six thousand dollars,'" he said. "And it's really not worth it. But I have new chrome and about two of every part as spares."

Next to the Studebaker was a Dodge. "It's a 1955 Dodge Royale," Sudberry said. "It has a V-8 with a trick-looking manifold. Just a grocery getter four-door, but another one that hasn't been molested. My dad bought that a long time ago, but I have no idea where."

The next car was an Olds 88. It was pretty well stripped out. "The guy I bought it from was going to put a big hot rod motor in it," he said. "Just another project car that never got finished. The front end is just wired on it to make it look better." Sudberry will take $1,500 for the Olds, which was a solid two-door.

On to his Cadillac, which is a 1953. "I bought it from one of Dad's friends, a pinstriper who lives about sixty-five or seventy miles from here," Sudberry said. "I think the guy still holds a quarter-mile record for some cubic-inch-size motorcycle class."

The Cadillac looked like a runner, but when Sudberry opened the hood, it had no engine or transmission. He said he has those items in the shed. "It's on eBay right now," he said. "I have an opening bid of fifteen hundred dollars. I know it's worth every bit of twenty-five hundred, which is a lot more than I have in it."

Before we left Sudberry's former gas station, he showed us a nice 1965 Ford Camper Special pickup, which looked to be totally original down to the paint, and with factory air conditioning. Sudberry told us, though, that it had been repainted years ago, and that the desert air and sun makes it look older than it is. "My father bought it in 1972," he said. I liked that truck.

Sudberry is working on a 1967 Mustang coupe. "This is one that I found on the Internet," he said. "I bought it because it has zero Bondo and zero floor rust. It only has surface rust all over it. The body lines are so straight and so good—not like most of the Mustangs you find. It's just a Plain Jane 289."

Sudberry said he plans to hot rod the car because it doesn't have a matching numbers drivetrain. It was well worth the $900 he paid for it. As we drove out of Sudberry's driveway, we drove directly across Route 66 and into our next "find." It was pretty obvious that whoever lived in that house liked Model A Fords.

ANY MODEL YOU LIKE, AS LONG AS IT'S A MODEL A

CAR COUNT	FOR SALE		
6	☐ Yes	★ No	☐ Maybe

We knocked on the door and met Gene Burke, who has lived on Route 66 in Truxton for fifteen years. "I like Model A Fords," he said. "I have everything from a 1928 to a 1931. Most of these I drove in here."

We walked over to a truck in his driveway. "This is a 1931," he said. "I bought it in Prescott about four years ago. I ran across it when I was down there."

Burke said he used to work on his old cars, but since turning seventy-four, the weather bothers him. He has lost his enthusiasm. "This truck is ready to start up and drive right now if I put in a battery and a radiator," he said.

Another car in Burke's driveway is his 1930 two-door sedan. "My buddy had this and he was working on it when he passed away, so I got it," he said. It was a pretty solid specimen for being eighty-five years old. "I used to make hot rods out of them back in the 1950s when I lived in Flagstaff. I put flathead V-8s in them. I had a '28 pickup like that one, but then I went into the army. Now my hot rodding days are over," Burke said.

Gene Burke is a lifelong Model A enthusiast. None of his cars are for sale. He enjoys when tourists, especially Europeans, knock on his door and ask him if they can take photos.

This 1931 Ford tow truck was purchased out of Prescott, Arizona. Burke also has AA trucks, chassis, and he said enough parts to build a Woody.

Gene Burke's driveway is nicely littered with all types of Model A Fords. Burke purchased this 1930 Tudor from the estate of a deceased friend.

This is what farmers used as tractors during the Great Depression. It's called a Doodlebug and was built out of a shortened Model A, usually an AA truck, which offered a two-speed differential.

We walked over to a Model A chassis he had next to the garage.

"I was going to make that one into a Woody, using that cowl over there," he said. "I have all the parts to put together a nice Woody. I buy parts at yard sales or wherever I can pick them up."

Burke said he likes the style of the Model A, and that they are easy to work on. "There are no electronic brains or anything like that."

Out front, he had a couple of more Model As, a Double AA truck, and a Double AA Doodlebug, which farmers used during the Great Depression instead of tractors. "It was a poor-man's tractor," he said. "If a man couldn't afford a tractor, he built one of these."

Burke said none of his vehicles are for sale. "I might not work on them, but if nothing else, I like to look at them."

Gene Burke is a salt-of-the earth car guy who loves when people stop by to talk about his old cars. "All summer long, Germans stop in here to talk about my cars and take pictures," he said.

Truxton was a productive little town for our group of barn-finders. We remained westbound on Route 66, which was rural and beautiful, all the way to Kingman, where we'd spend the night. As we approached our destination, we noticed a few old vehicles in the Golden Glory Trailer Park on the east side of town. We stopped, and as we walked around looking at the few old cars scattered about, a man approached us.

TRAILER PARK TREASURE

CAR COUNT
3

FOR SALE
☐ Yes ☐ No ⭐ Maybe

At first I thought he was crabby because of the colorful language he used, but the more time I spent with Henry Boatman, the more I liked him. Boatman owns the trailer park.

"I've lived here for forty-eight years," he said.

I asked him about a 1953 Ford Victoria in the back of his lot. "I've had that for about five years," he said. "Well it ain't mine. It's a long story. A couple was living here. I thought they were married, but they weren't. They moved to California with their camper and left the Ford here. Anyway, they broke up and he moved to Arkansas and got arrested and will be in jail for the rest of his life."

The car was in the woman's name, and Boatman hasn't heard from her in years. I asked him if the car still had the flathead V-8 in it. "No, it has some kind of different motor in it. It's not even hooked up," he said. I opened the hood and found either a 289 or 302 resting in the engine bay, but not bolted in.

Boatman had a "colorful vocabulary," but a heart of gold. His wife had recently passed away and he was learning to live without her.

Lights. Camera. Action. Behind the Golden Glory Trailer Park sat several cars, including this 1953 Ford Victoria. The original flathead had been removed and a 289 or 302 was installed in its place. Trailer park owner Henry Boatman cannot locate the owner, so it sits as Jordan and Ben record the interview.

When Boatman moved to Kingman, Arizona, from Minnesota, he drove this '51 Chevy 4x4 tow truck, complete with the snowplow. He sold the plow for scrap because it never snowed enough in his new home state.

Boatman told me about the 1949 Ford truck with the camper body.

"An old guy drove that in here and lived in it until he died," he said. "I ended up with it. That's how I get most of this stuff. I'm trying to peddle this stuff to a company in Golden Valley that buys 1950s and earlier cars. They came out here to look at this camper, but they weren't interested."

Boatman laughed when he told me that his trailer park used to be like Peyton Place, with an equal number of male and female residents. He said thankfully there are more couples living there now. Boatman moved to Kingman from Minnesota in 1968.

"I had a gas station in St. Paul," he said. "I was like an idiot when I moved here. I had a tow truck with a snowplow attached. I just cut the plow off a couple of years ago and scrapped it." He showed me the tow truck, which he still owned. It was a 1951 Chevy 4x4, and it was pretty rough. But it had been his for a half century, since he owned the gas station in St. Paul.

"Before the interstate went in, it would take ten minutes to cross the highway out front. Now, you could go into the middle of the road and take a nap."

Boatman gave me a business card, and it listed the owners of the Golden Glory Trailer Park as Henry and Millie Boatman. "Millie is dead," he said. "She died the seventeenth of last month. We were married for forty-one years. Now I'm by myself."

Now I understand why he seemed crabby when we first walked up. He was sad, lonely, and depressed. I followed Boatman into his house to get a form signed. The house was clean as a pin, vacuumed and neat. It was a wonderful to see how he was adjusting to his new life as a widower. I think Millie would be proud.

TRAILER PARK TREASURE, PART II

CAR COUNT
1

FOR SALE
★ Yes ■ No ■ Maybe

I asked Henry Boatman if he owned the fiberglass kit car next to one of the trailers. "No, that belongs to Dave Meredith," Boatman said. "He works at the post office and gets home around six o'clock."

I left a note in Meredith's door and asked if he'd give me a call. A few days later, we spoke.

"I've had that for about eight years," he said. "It's a Fiberfab Aztec GT. I'm a car guy, but I've never done any work on that car. I was living in another area and a neighbor had it. He found it in Mojave country. We were both going through divorces, so neither of us could afford to finish it."

Meredith noted that the car is a copy of a Ford GT40.

He had no idea why the rear half of the chassis is missing. "I think it was a running car at one time," he said. "But to restore it, the first step would be to get a new chassis. My hope would be to convert it to a Subaru drivetrain, to use modern technology."

But he mentioned that if someone offered him enough money, he would sell it. Unfortunately, we weren't in the market.

One of Boatman's tenants, Dave Meredith, owns this Fiberfab Aztec GT. Oddly, it is missing the rear half of the chassis, engine, and transmission. He said he would consider offers for the project car.

Route 66 Restorations had a slew of old cars—domestic, foreign, restored, and barn-find projects—all for sale. This Studebaker and El Camino were solid cars at reasonable prices.

Further into Kingman, we passed Route 66 Restorations, a shop that sold any type of old car, but specialized in restoring Mopar products. When the man working there, Curtis Neilson, saw my Woody, he said it looked familiar.

How could that be? He lives in Arizona and I live in North Carolina. Then he said, "Seven years ago my wife and I were on vacation in the Redwood Forest and we took a picture of a Woody driving through a giant redwood tree."

Amazing! My son Brian and I drove our Woody across the United States seven years ago and drove it through a giant redwood. Just another story of the road!

Neilson doesn't work on automobile restorations, but rents space to work on motorcycles. He said the owners of the restoration shop, Mike and Dave, were out of town, so we spoke to Curtis. "These are cars he has just picked up from the area," he said. "That old Cuda was dragged out of a sand wash where it was for ten or twelve years. The cab was smashed in, so

Rapid Gully Find: This Cuda was dragged out of a ditch and built into a rat rod drag car. Brown took it to the strip and ran in the thirteens!

they took a handyman jack and jacked the roof back into place, then cut Plexiglas for the windows."

He said they installed a 383, four-speed, and a rear end into the shell and took it to the strip. When they raced it, Neilson said it didn't even have door latches and "they turned the quarter-mile in the thirteens and won the 'Most Determined Award.'"

When I finally spoke to Dave Brown, owner of Route 66 Restorations, he said he has owned the business for eight years. "Mopars are my favorite," he said. "But I'll buy and restore anything. Yesterday I bought three 1940 Chevys."

He said that even though he owns dozens of cars, he still seeks a 1968 Plymouth Superbee. "I'd like a 383, four-speed in Forest Green, just like my older brother owned when I was a kid."

Route 66 Restorations owner Dave Brown said that his business specializes in Mopars, so he has the most of that brand. This 1966 Dodge Charger would be an ideal restoration candidate.

JUNK YARD GENTLEMAN

CAR COUNT	FOR SALE		
2,000+	★ Yes	☐ No	☐ Maybe

We had been told by people at least fifty miles east to be sure to visit Dan's Auto Salvage when we got to Kingman. So late that afternoon, we pulled into Dan's and met a nice young man just stepping into his truck. His name was Joseph Buchanan, and he was a third-generation junk yarder. His grandfather, Dan, started the business many years earlier, and his father runs it today. "I've been coming here since I was a little kid," said the twenty-year-old Buchanan.

Joseph Buchanan, the grandson of the founder, Dan, gave us a tour through the massive yard. Despite all these cars, he would like to find a Chevelle to restore.

We had been told by many people not to miss Dan's Auto Salvage in Kingman. We didn't have any problem finding it along Route 66, though. I never asked if they would consider selling the split windshield VW van that acted as the sign.

Probably the most scenic scrapyard in the world—junk cars, desert, mountain, and a speeding train.

Even though it was late in the afternoon on Friday (the 13th!), Buchanan said we could stay for a while and look around until he had to run off to the bank. "The best place to see the old cars is not here," he said. "Follow me to the other yard up the street. That's where the old stuff is."

I asked him if he had a favorite car. "Chevelles," he said without a moment's hesitation. "I don't have one right now, but my dad has a 1964 with a 502 big-block."

Buchanan told me his grandfather purchased this yard in 1988, but had two scrapyards prior to this one. We walked into the older part of the yard and were surrounded by hundreds of cars: old Ford trucks, a first-gen Barracuda, a 1954 or '55 Plymouth Plaza station wagon, a Plymouth Savoy,

Guys on the East Coast would kill to find a '57 Chevy this solid.

As the sun was going down, Michael got this great shot of a couple of Buicks: a 1955 and a Riviera.

You want old cars? Dan's doesn't have ten or twenty, but hundreds of old cars amongst thousands of later model wrecks. Check out this solid and complete 1955 Plymouth Plaza wagon.

a Chevelle, a 1959 Buick. There were rows and rows of cars, all solid and many worthy of restoration. We walked past a couple of Gremlins, which Buchanan said will fit a big-block Chevy engine. Then we saw a couple of 1957 Chevys, Pintos, a Corvair, and an Olds Toronado.

He said if we walked across the railroad tracks and over the sand berm, another section of the junkyard had lots of Mustangs, Novas, and so forth. Those cars, he said, were mostly good for parts cars. I asked if there were rattlesnakes around. "Yes, in the summer, especially on the other side of the tracks," he said. Which is where we were heading. Yikes!

Buchanan said his family owns about 70 acres, including the mountain in the distance. A mountain!

Look at the condition of this row of Fords: a 1953 Lincoln and a 1959 and 1953 Victoria. Dan's grandson, Joseph Buchanan, took us for a tour around acres and acres of cars, all of which are for sale.

I asked Buchanan how many cars all three sections of their yards contained. He estimated five thousand, of which about two thousand would have some kind of collector interest. That's a lot of vehicles.

Our Hagerty video team, Jordan and Ben, as well as Michael, were all intrigued with photographing the Buchanan's mountain in the distance. They asked if it would be OK if they stayed here to photograph and video the sunset. He said it would not be a problem. Surrounded by fields of junk cars, it was probably the most beautiful evening of our trip. Not a bad Friday the Thirteenth.

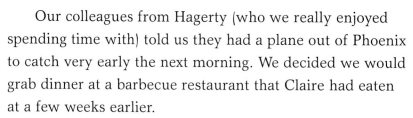

Oatman is an amazing town. Even though it is somewhat Disney like, it is a real old town, with real old businesses, such as the Oatman Hotel, built in 1902.

Our colleagues from Hagerty (who we really enjoyed spending time with) told us they had a plane out of Phoenix to catch very early the next morning. We decided we would grab dinner at a barbecue restaurant that Claire had eaten at a few weeks earlier.

After the sun had set and the photographing and videotaping was completed, the five of us converged on Redneck's Southern Pit BBQ in Kingman and had a terrific time. The food was amazing and their local craft brew selection was top-notch. After a wonderful meal and lots of conversation about the past four days, we said goodbye to Claire, Jordon, and Ben, our barn-find traveling companions, who were heading south toward Phoenix.

With any luck, the videos that the Hagerty crew shot across New Mexico and Arizona were good enough to be included in their electronic newsletter (Google "Barnfind Hunter".) Michael and I said goodbye and watched them drive off. We didn't envy them because they had a four-hour drive to Phoenix, probably arriving at 1 a.m., then had to catch a 6 a.m. flight to begin the long slog to Traverse City, Michigan.

Before we left Dan's, my Hagerty colleagues wanted to use the beautiful setting sun to do a final interview before we all left for a wonderful barbecue dinner at Redneck's in Kingman.

The goodwill ambassadors in Oatman are burros that have the run of the town. Like towns that allow tourists to feed the geese or the deer, stores in Oatman sell burro feed to tourists.

We were getting closer! I-40 runs from North Carolina (where I live) almost all the way to Los Angeles, 2,553 miles all the way. Michael and I decided to go west.

We decided to take a selfie while we were both still in Arizona. After fourteen days on the road, we were about to enter California, the eighth state on our Route 66 adventure.

We hit the hotel for a good night's sleep. We would be entering our last state, California, about an hour after leaving our hotel in the morning. With any luck, in another day-and-a-half, we'll be standing on the Santa Monica Pier. Good night, Kingman.

◆ SATURDAY, NOVEMBER 14, 2015 ◆

The night before, I asked Joseph Buchanan where Ford's test track was located. He said about 40 miles west of town. I assumed it was located on Route 66, but we never did locate the track as we traveled west toward the California border.

The Route 66 town of Oatman had some of the most dramatic scenery we had seen yet. We traversed twisty mountain passes with sheer drop-offs and few if any guardrails. The scenery was amazing; I know that Michael could have spent a day shooting photos there. It was about 11 a.m. when he mentioned, "This place would be amazing at around four o'clock."

Not this time, Michael. We had miles to make.

CHAPTER 8

ROUTE 66

CALIFORNIA

Crossing into California became a significant event as it marked the last state of the Route 66 Barn Find Road Trip. In some small way, I felt I knew what early Route 66 travelers must have felt like when they reached California in order to start a new life.

• • • • • • • •

The first town in our last state was Needles. Prior to arriving here, the only thing I ever knew about Needles was that it was where *Peanuts* character Snoopy's older brother Spike lived. In the cartoon, it seemed like a pretty flat desert, and the cartoon wasn't kidding. It *was* a pretty flat desert with the occasional fast food place or gas station thrown in to give the landscape some texture.

ALASKAN BARN-FINDER

CAR COUNT 9	FOR SALE ★ Yes ■ No ■ Maybe

It was at one of those gas stations where we found some unusual cars on a parked car hauling trailer. These included two 1955 (I think) Plymouths—one a wagon, which is pretty rare—a 1950 Ford Woody, and two GM products, a 1952 Chevy station wagon, and a 1948 Chevy Sedan Delivery.

I asked the gas station attendant about who owned the cars and he told me Tom Nelson, who also owned Route 66 Tool Rentals on Front Street. We drove to the rental store a few miles away and met Nelson.

The first "major" town we reached in California was Needles. I had only heard about that before because it was where Snoopy's brother Spike lived . . .

Excuse me for including so many station wagons in this book, but I love them! Station wagons and trucks were usually beat up and thrown away, so nice examples are rare. Asking price for this '56 Plymouth Sport Suburban and parts car is $5,000.

This 1950 Ford woodless Woody came from Alaska. Wood body kits are readily available, as are trim and hard parts. Tom Nelson will let it go for $3,500, a fair price for a complete, solid car.

Tom Nelson is an interesting guy: railroad worker, hot rodder, Alaskan pioneer, and the new owner of a Dodge Hellcat. He also owns a bunch of cool old iron.

"I dragged two woodies, that '52 Chevy, and a '50 Ford out of a barn that had collapsed around them in Alaska," he said. "I had been talking to the guy about buying them before the barn collapsed. It was outside of Wasilla. The guy wanted a ridiculous amount for them before the barn fell, like ten thousand dollars each. After it collapsed, he told us if we dug them out, we could have them for one thousand each."

He said the "tin woody," the Chevy, had pretty good metal on it. But the Ford was pretty well gone.

Nelson lives in Needles and works full time for the railroad, but he keeps a house in Wasilla, Alaska, where he hopes to retire. He returns there often, to look for old cars.

Nelson told me about hauling the woodies back from Alaska: "When I was hauling them through Canada, a guy came up to me and said, 'You should see what I've got. I've got a car you need to look at.'"

Nelson resurrected this 1952 Chevy "metal" Woody from a collapsed Alaska barn. It looked pretty good and the $3,500 asking price was fair, especially considering the solid condition.

Nelson said he tried his best to discourage the guy, but the man insisted. "I followed him into the middle of nowhere Canada," Nelson said, "and he had that '48 Chevy Sedan Delivery that I have parked near the highway. It has factory side windows," he said. "I was told that it hauled nitroglycerine for a mining company. It runs but has one wheel locked up. I'm asking ten thousand dollars for that, but have a little flexibility."

This '48 Chevy sedan delivery, at $10,000, was on the high side of value, considering a full restoration was required. It certainly was a solid starting point, though.

He told us about a hot rod project he was building from an old Chevy he bought in Oatman, Arizona, the town we had just visited the day before. "It's a 1931 Chevy five-window pickup truck," he said. "A friend of mine bought it, then got bit by a spider and died, so I bought it from his widow. It's being painted now, but it will have a Hilborn fuel-injected 427 and a chassis stretched nineteen inches. It started out as a coupe, so the proportions look correct as a truck."

He said the Plymouth wagon came from Needles. It's a 1956 Plymouth Sport Suburban, similar to the one that appeared in the movie, *The World's Fastest Indian*. This wagon is a four-door with a six-cylinder and a cast-iron Torqueflite automatic.

"I actually had the wagon sold to a dentist back east," Nelson said. "He sent me a check, then got a divorce, so his wife cancelled the check. So we have kind of been in limbo for five years."

Nelson's plans for this '40 Plymouth coupe are to make it a gasser-type of street car, with a straight front axle and a blown Hemi engine that once powered a competitor Don Garlits's dragster!

He'd like to get $5,000 for the wagon and a sedan parts car. For the two woodies, the '52 Chevy, and the '50 Ford, he'd like to get $3,500 each.

He showed me a 1940 Plymouth business gasser coupe with a straight front axle and a blown 392 Hemi that has been detuned to about 650 horsepower. "That engine has a history," he said. "It put out eighteen-hundred-

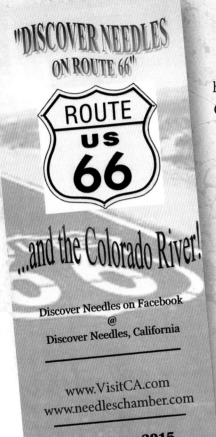

horsepower and raced in a slingshot rail dragster against Don Garlits back in the day. The Plymouth had been drag-raced in the Kingman area with a 350 Chevy. It's a project that is taking a lot longer than I ever thought."

Nelson showed us an amphibious truck. "It's a 1964 M1-316 Husky and it floats," he said. "It's a war surplus. I rebuilt the transmission, so now I just need to put it back together. It's aluminum and has bilge pumps because it barely floats."

Nelson had been into old cars since he was a kid. Needles was too good a town to leave quickly. We cruised around for a while because we sensed more cars in the area. For instance, we saw two interesting cars in a yard, a 1955 Ford Wagon with a four-speed and a 1940-ish Oldsmobile sedan. They were authentic old cars, solid, and not restored. They looked to be daily drivers.

I knocked on the door and nobody answered. Nuts! So I left a note in the door and hoped for a call in a day or so. Sadly, I never heard from the owners of those cars.

TAKE CARE TO TAKE CARE

Barn-finding is not a clean business. In fact, it can be downright filthy.

Be prepared to walk through waist-high weeds, sticker bushes, swampy water, mosquitos, and spikey little balls that attach themselves to your pants, socks, and shoes.

And when you try to brush those spikey little balls off with your hand, you get stabbed in the fingers with porcupine-like needles. (They are best removed by "flicking" them off with a pocketknife.)

Depending on where you are hunting, it's best to wear work clothes you don't care about. Try leather boots (never sandals), blue jeans (never shorts), and a denim long-sleeve shirt.

Take it from a guy who, at sixteen years old, walked through a junkyard barefoot *and* with shorts(!). At sixty-one, I still have the scar on my left thigh from the stab wound I received from a piece of stainless steel that pierced my flesh and left a 2-inch gash.

We headed west from Needles toward Barstow. Nelson told us we were about three hours from Barstow, California, if we drove on Route 66. But one thing we hadn't planned on was the rough road surface.

In eastern California, Route 66 was closed off for many miles with signs that read "Road Closed," "Detour," and "Impassible." So we had to drive many miles on I-40 from Essex (Exit 107) to Amboy (Exit 78).

When we were able to enter Route 66 again, I wished we never had. The sun was setting, but the beautiful sky was offset by the horrible road surface. In some places the road was so rough that it would have been much better suited for a late-model F-150 Ford pickup than a seventy-six-year-old Woody.

The body on my car—which is screwed together—was creaking and rattling worse than I've ever heard before. And in the dark, with headlights that are marginal at best, I was slamming potholes and bottoming out the suspension. I took the first opportunity to re-enter I-40 and we continued our journey west toward Barstow.

Michael and I arrived in Barstow, checked into our hotel, and went out to have a nice dinner. We discovered Napoli's and had a wonderful pizza and craft beer. Perfect end to a perfect day (except for the potholes, of course). Tomorrow was the last day of our journey.

◆ SUNDAY, NOVEMBER 15, 2015 ◆

We hoped to find at least a few cars today, the last of our fifteen-day adventure of driving Route 66 from beginning to end.

Michael suggested we visit El Mirage, a dry lake where hot rods occasionally make record runs. Today was the last speed record session of the season. We thought that perhaps we could get a couple of leads from racers there, plus we could see some cool cars driving fast. I have never been to Bonneville or any place like that before, so I was stoked.

But even though the day dawned sunny and clear, it was terribly windy. It took two hands on the wheel in a death grip to keep the Woody driving straight down the road. As we grew closer to El Mirage, the wind became more and more severe. It appeared we were driving into a fog bank.

It was a sandstorm.

I told Michael that if we go to that dry lake, we'll need new paint jobs on both the Woody and the Ford Explorer. He agreed, and we turned around. I hope to visit there sometime on a less turbulent day.

We saw some vintage tin at ranches and houses along the road, but I couldn't bring myself to knock on anybody's door that early on a Sunday morning. But as we drove down the road, we both noticed some old cars parked behind a fence. It was only about 9 a.m. and there were people standing in the yard. It didn't look like they were getting ready to go to church, so I decided to take a chance, turned the wheel, and drove up the driveway. I walked up to the guys and introduced myself. They were totally cool, and in fact enthusiastic that we were there.

That's the magic of the Woody.

SUNDAY MORNING PARTIERS

CAR COUNT	FOR SALE
7	Yes ★No Maybe

The guys who made our Sunday morning barn-finding easy: (from left to right) Scott Allen, Mike Lee, and Rick Stidham. These guys, who were feeling no pain, were still partying from the night before!

It didn't take me long to realize that these guys were "feeling no pain." They were the perfect people to approach on a Sunday morning—they hadn't gone to sleep yet from Saturday night!

"Come on in, guys," said a gentleman named Mike Lee, the spokesman for the group. "We're glad you are here. This is totally cool."

OK, I admit it: this Nash was my singular favorite car of the trip, this 1949 or '50 Nash. I love the body style and the condition. If owner Don Wilson would sell the car, I would own it right now. And install an LS drivetrain.

Lee and Scott Allen, Rick Stidham, and a guy who wouldn't identify himself are tenants at the house, and their landlord owned the cars we were interested in.

"Look at anything you want," Lee said as he was opening another Budweiser, offering one to Michael and me.

"No thanks," I said. "I haven't even digested my pancakes yet."

These guys were fun-loving and each had an interesting story to tell. They lived on a several-acre lot in the town of Oro Grande. Scattered around their yard were a number of cars, and most in pretty darn solid condition There was a fiberglass

A bunch of old cars always get our attention, but on a Sunday morning with a bunch of guys hanging around them, it was downright exciting. Strange bedfellows are this dune buggy and a 1956 Clipper.

dune buggy, a '56 Packard Clipper, a '63 Ford Thunderbird, the world's only StudeVette (I'll explain later), and my favorite, a Nash Statesman Custom, probably a 1950.

I called their landlord, Don Wilson. Wilson has been a car guy since he was a kid. He told me the story about his first auto repair. "My father had a 1946 Ford, and the rear end went out, so he just parked it," Wilson said, who retired from Lockheed after thirty years. "I was about eleven or twelve years old, and I fixed that car."

Wilson bought a 1966 Ford 7-liter Galaxie brand new, sold it in 1971, and then found it and bought it back again ten years later. He restored it and still owns it today. I asked him about a couple of his cars we found along Route 66 in Oro Grande, California. For instance, that weird StudeVette.

"I saw an ad for that in the Lake Havasu area," he said. "I paid about eighteen hundred dollars for it. It was built from a 1955 Studebaker Golden

This 1963 Thunderbird was a pretty neat car. My very first model kit for my eighth birthday from my friend Buzzy Brischler was a 1963 Thunderbird, so I always have a soft spot in my heart for the model.

Hawk, had a 1980 Camaro nose installed, a T-Bird roof and seats, and a 1958 Corvette rear section. It is powered by a Chevy 350. I saw a snapshot of the car when it was completed, and it looked pretty good at one time."

Wilson said he originally toyed with the idea of converting it to a drag car, but now is unsure of exactly what to do with it. I told Wilson that the car I was most

The oddest vehicle we found on the trip was this StudeVette. It's part Studebaker, part Camaro, part Corvette, and part T-bird, all wrapped up in one questionable package.

attracted to was the Nash. "I'm still not sure what to do with that car," he said, "although I will probably leave the patina the way it is." He told me he has an LS1 drivetrain that could go right into that Nash. "I just love the style," he said.

I do too. I asked if he would consider selling it, and he shut that door pretty quickly. "I hardly sell anything," he said. "I buy them and I build them the way I like. I'm putting up a new forty-foot-by-eighty-foot building to store my cars."

Wilson promised to send me photos when the Nash is completed. This turned out to be a terrific discovery, and the guys who rent Wilson's house were fun to hang out with and were extremely helpful, especially when they agreed to move the Nash 180 degrees for a better photo location.

"Wow, when you guys drove that Woody up the driveway, you made our day," Lee said as we got into our cars to leave.

By the time we left our friends in Oro Grande, the time was ticking away. After fifteen days on the road, we were just hours away from completing our journey at the Santa Monica Pier, southwest of LA.

Before we headed to the pier, we had to follow up a lead we couldn't pass up. There was one more car to uncover—possibly the most significant car of all—and certainly the best car to end this book.

A SNAKE IN THE GRASS

CAR COUNT	FOR SALE
1	☐ Yes ★ No ☐ Maybe

In a town I promised not to identify I met a man who wished to remain anonymous who owns a 289 Cobra that I can't reveal the serial number of . . .

The man, who we'll just call "Guy," has owned the Cobra for decades. He paid only a few thousand dollars for it more than forty years ago. He drove it with vigor for many years, but these days it is buried in his garage.

This car is a late serial number 289 Cobra with rack-and-pinion steering. And it can certainly never be accused of being a trailer queen—Guy brags about the fact that he used to use Krylon spray paint to touch up scratches and stone dings.

"I bought this car in the early seventies," Guy said. "It was from the back of *Road and Track* magazine. Because I was a subscriber, I got the magazine one week ahead of the newsstand. I was twenty-six and had no means to buy it. The owner wanted sixty-five hundred dollars. I offered him six thousand and he said yes. So I scrounged up six thousand, put the cash in a sock, and flew to Seattle, where the seller picked me up. We went out for a test drive—where he scared the bejesus out of me—and by the time we got back to his house, there were envelopes that had arrived in his mail, all from people who wanted to buy the Cobra. One envelope had a sixty-five hundred dollar check, the other seven thousand, and seventy-five hundred."

Our last find, and our best. This genuine 289 Cobra has been buried in this garage for many years. The owner, who bought it in the early 1970s, is not interested in discussing a sale. But, oh, boy, it is cool. Take it from a lifelong Cobra enthusiast.

We made it! Fifteen days and nearly 3,000 miles, this seventy-six-year-old car made it from Chicago without any mechanical issues! It was a great day and a great trip. I'd do it again in a heartbeat!

But the man stood by his deal and sold the car to the enthusiastic twenty-six-year-old. "I-5 had just opened up from Canada to Mexico, and it was very smooth and clear, so I drove one thousand one hundred miles in nineteen hours," Guy said.

Is he interested in selling the car? "No," he said. "In fact, hell no! I love this car as much now as when I bought it."

I admire his attitude. He bought the car because he loved it, and now— forty years later— the car approaching seven figures in value, he has no interest in selling. And neither would I.

We said goodbye and headed to Santa Monica, the last leg of our adventure. Before Michael and I pulled the Woody onto the pier, we wondered what we'd experience. We hoped there would be a crowd of people waving their hands, confetti cannons blazing, maybe a brass band cheering us for our Route 66 accomplishment.

◆ END OF THE ROUTE 66 BARN FIND ROAD TRIP ◆

ENDING MILEAGE: 27,782 MILES
TOTAL MILEAGE: 3,133 MILES

Instead, what we heard was: "Hey, buddy, move that car! NOW!"

One of Santa Monica's finest shouted orders to us as we entered the pier. Michael jumped out so he could take photos of the Woody in front of the "Route 66 End" sign.

"Hey, did you hear what I said?" screamed the police officer.

Obviously this guy hadn't heard about our Route 66 tour. Michael explained to him that we were just completing an adventure of the entire length of Route 66.

No good. "I said move that car, or I'll have it towed."

Despite the officer's rants, Michael was able to grab a couple of shots. But we got the message. We drove into the

It's official! And this sign proves it. Now it was time for a beer!

Remember that bottle of water I retrieved from Lake Michigan? Well, we took care of it for nearly 3,000 miles, and here I am dumping it into the Pacific Ocean. I was waiting for some crabby police officer to come over and arrest me . . .

The only vehicle casualty was this broken headlight lens, which must have collected a stone somewhere on our trip. No big deal. I live near Dennis Carpenter's shop in Concord, North Carolina, so a replacement would be a piece of cake.

I want to give a shoutout to my friend and photographer partner in these books, Michael Alan Ross. Michael endured all my crazy ideas, trudged through weeds and mud, and made probably hundreds of U-turns when I saw old cars we had just passed. Thank you, Michael. You are one of the top automotive photographers in the industry; why are you shooting rust?

parking area and grabbed our cameras (like common tourists!) and shot photos of that famous sign. Then we sought out the official Route 66 shop on the pier to buy t-shirts and other official tchotchkes from the Mother Road.

◆ SAY GOODNIGHT, JAY . . . ◆

The next morning we drove to Jay Leno's Big Dog Garage, in Burbank, for a quick visit. Jay and I have been friends for many years, and he was intrigued with our trip and wanted to know if we found any great cars.

And I wanted to check on the Cunningham C-3 I sold him two years earlier. Jay and his crew were nearing the end of a thorough restoration and it was looking beautiful. I'm looking forward to the car's restoration being completed—it will be a good excuse to make another West Coast trip!

Well, we were done. When we left Grant Park in Chicago, the Woody's odometer read 24,649 miles. When we arrived at the Santa Monica Pier, the odometer read 27,782, which means we completed 3,133 miles on one of the world's most iconic roads, found thousands of cool old cars, met incredible people, and saw amazing sights.

How many cars? I never would have believed it, but 7,901 cars and trucks (give or take a few hundred) because some of those larger scrapyards were estimates by the owners. The actual number could be higher or lower. These were cars actually found on or near Route 66.

Fini.

We had just completed the trip of a lifetime, a journey that a million other people would love to have joined us on. I'm not sure about Michael or Brian, but if I made that trip again, two and one half weeks is just not enough time. A month seems more like it.

As I sit at my desk and put the finishing touches on this manuscript before it ships to the publisher, I feel satisfied, yet anxious. Our Route 66 Road Trip was just a couple of months ago, but I miss the constant din of the Woody's exhaust. I even miss the strong cross drafts that whipped around the car's interior. But more than anything else, I miss the amazing car people we met and the cars we discovered.

How many cars we saw behind locked gates might have a great story to tell. Or might be for sale?

If I had taken a left turn instead of a right turn in some of those small towns, would we have discovered something truly amazing?

How many more cars would we have discovered IF we had driven from west to east instead of east to west?

I have the feeling that a return engagement is in order.

The road calls.

Santa Monica may have been the official end of our tour, but a visit to friend Jay Leno's shop was my personal finish line. Jay loves barn-find cars and would love to join us on a future adventure if his time allowed.

POSTSCRIPT I

It took fifteen days to travel from Chicago to LA, finding old cars and interviewing their owners along the way. But I needed to get back to Chicago in only three days in order to participate in a book signing at the Muscle Car and Corvette Nationals for the first book in this series, *Barn Find Road Trip*. That poor Woody spent three days driving at 70 to 80 miles per hour for hours on end. One day I drove 1,000 miles!

When my good friend Woody Woodruff (not to be confused with my car, also called Woody) heard that I would be traveling back east by myself, he decided a road trip for two sounded better than one. So he volunteered to meet me in Flagstaff, Arizona, and drive with me back to Chicago, then Charlotte.

What a pal. Woody always comes through when I need help, and I appreciate it so much. So Woody jumped on an Amtrak train and arrived in Flagstaff after a four-day journey, at about 1 a.m. on Wednesday morning. I picked him up, we grabbed a few hours' sleep in the local Hampton Inn, then hit the road hard for the next few days.

As we were approaching Gallup, New Mexico, I thought it would be a good idea to visit Alvin Yellowhorse, the jewelry designer and barn-find collector on the Navajo reservation just along the interstate. I thought that because Christmas was only one month away, I would buy my wife, Pat, a nice piece of custom Indian jewelry. But a funny thing happened on the way to the jewelry studio: the steering in the Woody got tough just as I entered the exit ramp. As I looked at the gauges, I noticed that the alternator was not charging. Hmm.

For those who read *Barn Find Road Trip*, you might remember that I had some issues with my car's belt-drive system. "Oh, boy, "I thought, "here we go again."

Yellowhorse's studio was only a couple of hundred feet from the exit. So I drove there and walked into his studio.

His work is fabulous—absolutely museum quality. He showed me his products and explained that he bought the best stones and minerals on earth, such as the burned-orange coral and turquoise he was currently working with.

"But I don't sell my jewelry retail," he said. "I have agents who sell my items in New York, Chicago, and Europe."

He showed me a beautiful bracelet and I inquired about its cost. "That sells for eight thousand dollars retail," he said.

Yikes! I guess Pat wasn't going to get *that* bracelet for Christmas. I thanked him and said that his pieces were beautiful, but out of my price range.

As we walked out to my car, I told Yellowhorse that my steering and alternator was acting up, and that I needed to find a garage. "Bring it over to my garage," he said, which was right next door.

We quickly diagnosed the Woody with a broken adjustment bolt that snapped off in the cylinder head. Yellowhorse drilled and used an easy-out to withdraw the broken bolt, then rethreaded a Grade 8 bolt to the correct metric thread and pitch. What could have been a lost day was simply a two-hour delay before we were back on the road.

Thank you, Alvin Yellowhorse. One day I hope to be able to afford one of your fine pieces of jewelry for Pat.

This experience was further proof that any barn-find road trip is really about the people, not the cars, and their experiences and stories to share.

Beyond the scenery and the cars, the most wonderful part of the trip was meeting the people. We were complete strangers who spoke to hundreds of automotive enthusiasts—ex-racers, collectors, keepers of family heirlooms. And in every case, we treated as equals and as friends.

Car people are amazing, whether they live north, south, east, or west. It's as if we are all part of a secret fraternity and know the secret handshake. I am not aware of another group of folks who have this amazing bond. I worked in the auto racing industry for twenty-five years, have been a businessman and an educator, and in none of those professions have I experienced the same sense of instant friendship that I have in the old car world.

If car guys ran the country in this age of bipartisan politics and television shouting sessions, I wonder if things might go a bit smoother. At the very least, I bet we'd have smoother roads, higher speed limits, and calmer discussions around a couple of beers when the sun begins to set—it's 5 o'clock somewhere!

See you down the road.

—Tom

BEST-OFs

FOOD
BEST HOT DOG: Wiener Circle, Chicago, Illinois
BEST FROZEN CUSTARD: Ted Drewes, St. Louis, Missouri
BEST TACO: Prime Taco, St. Louis, Missouri
BEST BURGER: Happy Burger, Sapulpa, Oklahoma
BEST DONUT: The Donut Stop, Amarillo, Texas
BEST DINNER: Stuffed Quail, Hoffbrau Steakhouse, Amarillo, Texas
BEST BARBECUE: Redneck's Southern Pit Barbecue, Kingman, Arizona

PLACES
BEST VINTAGE GAS STATION: Standard Oil Station/Museum, Odell, Illinois
BEST ROADHOUSE: The Elbow Inn, Devil's Elbow, Missouri
MOST IMPRESSIVE TECHNOLOGY: Wind Farms of Western Oklahoma and Texas
BEST ROADSIDE ATTRACTION: Cadillac Ranch, Amarillo, Texas
BEST ROAD SEGMENT: Route 66 toward Oatman, Arizona

PEOPLE
BEST, FRIENDLIEST SERVER: Tanya McCarter, The Palms Grill Café, Atlanta, Illinois
BEST CHARACTERS/PERSONALITIES: Archie Lewis, Lewis Auto and Toy Museum, Moriarty, New Mexico, and John Hargrove, Arcadia, Oklahoma
BEST GOOD SAMARITAN: Kathy Alexander, Oklahoma State Police, Clinton, Oklahoma
BEST BARTENDER: Schuyler Cochran, Hoffbrau Steakhouse, Amarillo Texas
BEST SOCIAL MEDIA TIP: Jim Goodman (Michael's high school classmate) who turned us onto Boomer's salvage yard in Albuquerque, New Mexico
BEST DOG: Dutch, at Alvin Yellowtail's repair shop, Gallup, New Mexico
BEST CONFESSIONAL (GUARANTEED TO RECEIVE ABSOLUTION): Buying a raffle ticket for the restored 1972 454 Chevelle from Father Matt Keller at Sacred Heart Cathedral, Gallup, New Mexico

LAST BUT NOT LEAST—
THE BEST CARS OF THE ROUTE 66 BARN FIND ROAD TRIP
MOST UNUSUAL CAR LOCATION: Crosley race car in an upstairs bedroom, Danvers, Illinois
BEST PROFESSIONAL/SERVICE CAR: Packard Ambulance, Tulsa, Oklahoma
MOST UNUSUAL CAR: Shark-nosed supercharged Graham, Tucumcari, New Mexico
BEST CELEBRITY OWNERSHIP: 1961 Lincoln Continental of Ella Fitzgerald, Albuquerque, New Mexico
BEST TRUCK: Autocar COE fuel tanker, Albuquerque, New Mexico

CARS WE WANT THE MOST
TOM COTTER: 1950 Nash Statesman Custom, Oro Grand, California
MICHAEL ALAN ROSS: The same 1950 Nash Statesman Custom
BRIAN BARR: AF/X Dart or belly-tanker, Chuck's Towing Service, Joplin, Missouri

INDEX